I SHALL NOT WANT

An Exposition of Psalm Twenty-three

by
R. T. KETCHAM

MOODY PRESS • CHICAGO

Contents

Foreword

THE WRITER of this booklet has walked with the Shepherd more than two score years. It will become evident that his instructions come out of the fiery furnace of affliction. He has proved the faithfulness of the Shepherd.

Because it is my privilege to know him so well, I count it a great privilege to pen this introduction. Dr. Ketcham is a sincere Christian, a man deeply taught of God, a superlative preacher. Standing for the faith unflinchingly, so that opponents quail before the incisiveness of his logical thrusts of eloquence, he nevertheless has the heart of a child— he loves the Lord Jesus and his brethren. Tears have mellowed him. Heartaches have strengthened him. Disaster has only made him lean harder on the Lord.

Burdened with executive responsibility that would sink many a younger man (he travels close to fifty thousand miles a year, delivers major addresses more in number each year than there are days in the year, keeps up a voluminous correspondence, coedits a paper, and gives of his heart to thousands—accomplishing all this in spite of very poor eyesight), the Shepherd has taught him the secret of the springs of hidden strength.

We introduce him—not merely as a great preacher, nor only as occupying a very important administrative position in his denomination (National Representative, General Association of Regular Baptist Churches), but as a humble Christian taught of God. This undershepherd has been on ahead of many of us; he has discovered some wonderful truths about the great Shepherd. And here he has come back to the rest of us to tell us what he has found so that we may go ahead with confidence, for the Shepherd is there to meet us too if we will but follow.

William Culbertson

July, 1953

Preface

THESE MESSAGES on the Twenty-third Psalm have, over a period of several years, been delivered to the congregations of my own churches and to many summer Bible conferences. They were condensed into a series of five messages and delivered before the Moody Founder's Week conference in February, 1953. Because of constant requests to put these messages into book form, it has been decided to do so. They are sent forth with the earnest prayer that the readers will receive some of the blessing which has been the portion of the visible audiences and, above all, something of the blessing which has come to the heart of the author in his preparation and delivery of them.

Acknowledgment is hereby made of much help from many sources on this psalm. Many writers and teachers have contributed to my knowledge and understanding of the psalm. However, my richest source of blessing has been found in the school of experience through which the Shepherd Himself has led me. Much may be learned from other men's books—infinitely more may be learned as one, for himself and by himself, walks through the shadows and the sunshine alone with the Shepherd.

The literary style is not altogether satisfactory, due to the fact that the manuscript is a reproduction of the expositions as given orally in public addresses. An endeavor has been made to capture from the tape recordings something of the extemporaneous character of these addresses and at the same time impart to the manuscript a style which makes the book easily readable.

1

An Introduction to the Psalm

THERE IS PERHAPS no more familiar passage of Scripture than the Twenty-third Psalm. It is one of the earliest extended portions committed to memory in childhood. Verse 1 of the psalm presents a very present help in time of trouble when, on prayer meeting night, the pastor suddenly asks his congregation for a verse of Scripture. Immediately someone will spring up and say, "The LORD is my shepherd, I shall not want," before someone else can get to it.

It is this very familiarity with the psalm which constitutes its peril. Someone has said, "Familiarity breeds contempt." I assume that this is intended to indicate that either appreciation of or dislike for certain situations may be gradually modified by constant association. Certainly long familiarity with a passage of Scripture, such as the Twenty-third Psalm, may cause one to lose the keen edge of appreciation and just take it for granted. This has been the fate of this wonderful portion of Scripture at the hands of thousands of really born-again believers.

During nearly sixty years in the ministry I have

heard hundreds of people quote the first verse of
Psalm 23 even though it was obvious that the
verse had almost no application to their daily experience. They could quote the words, "The LORD
is my shepherd; I shall not want," but I knew their
life was a wilderness of "want." What they really
meant was, "The Lord is my *Saviour,* and I am glad
He is." They had failed utterly to realize that there
is a vast difference between the *saviourhood* of
Jesus Christ and the *shepherdhood* of Jesus Christ.
One may know the Lord as *Saviour* and know almost nothing of Him as *Shepherd,* as revealed in
this marvelous psalm.

The New Testament presents the Lord Jesus as
exercising a threefold shepherd ministry. In John
10:11 He calls Himself the "good shepherd" and
declares that "the good shepherd giveth his life for
the sheep." In Hebrews 13:20 the inspired writer
calls the Lord "that great shepherd of the sheep"
and says that He became the great Shepherd
through being "brought again from the dead." In
1 Peter 5:4 the Lord Jesus is called "the chief
shepherd" and Peter declares that He becomes the
chief Shepherd in His second advent when He shall
give to His own "a crown of glory that fadeth not
away."

Here, then, the Lord Jesus is placed before us as
the good Shepherd, the great Shepherd, and the
chief Shepherd. As the good Shepherd, He *dies*
for the sheep. As the great Shepherd, He *lives* for
the sheep. As the chief Shepherd, He *comes* for the
sheep.

It is the relationship of the *good Shepherd* to the sheep rather than the relationship of the great Shepherd to the sheep that is referred to by many people when they quote verse 1 of Psalm 23. They are thinking of the ministry of the good Shepherd who died for them on Calvary's cross, and who, for that matter, is also living in heaven and whom they are sure they will meet someday. The glorious truth that they should be meeting Him *every day* in green pastures and beside still waters has never dawned upon them, or at least has never become a blessed, daily experience in their Christian life. True it is that one cannot know Christ as *Shepherd* without knowing Him as *Saviour,* but the tragedy is that born-again believers who know Him as Saviour may never know Him in their daily experience as a blessed present Shepherd.

This threefold shepherd ministry of Christ is beautifully set forth in the triplet psalms, namely, Psalms 22, 23 and 24. Psalm 22 presents Him as the good Shepherd in death. Psalm 23 presents Him as the great Shepherd in life. Psalm 24 presents Him as the chief Shepherd in His sure return.

The opening sentence of Psalm 22 is the very dictation of Calvary's cry of rejection—"My God, my God, why hast thou forsaken me?" These words are not primarily a quotation from Matthew 27:46, but Matthew 27:46 is the Lord Jesus Himself quoting from Psalm 22:1—quoting in awful, literal and terrible fulfillment all of the black and overwhelming portent of these words!

Psalm 22 is a literal word picture of the experiences of death by crucifixion; but more than that, *the death of the Son of God* by crucifixion. Even the details of garments parted, lots cast upon vesture, and pierced hands and feet, are here laid bare before us. Surely this is the good Shepherd giving His life for His sheep.

I cannot accept the view that Psalm 22 has reference to a particular, personal experience of David. There are some things in this psalm which David never experienced. For instance, look at verses 16 and 18, "They pierced my hands and my feet. . . . They part my garments among them, and cast lots upon my vesture." This was never done to David. I recognize that in many of the prophetic psalms there is a near and a remote fulfillment. For instance, when David said in Psalm 41:9, "Mine own familiar friend, in whom I trusted, which did eat of my bread, hath lifted up his heel against me", he certainly was referring to his own experience. But in John 13:18 we discover that the Lord Jesus Christ reaches back over the centuries and lifts that little, almost forgotten, expression of David out of its ancient setting, and says "that the scripture may be fulfilled, He that eateth bread with me hath lifted up his heel against me," and applied it to His experience with Judas. In this case the great camera focus in this prophecy was not directed particularly on David. He was simply caught on the sidelines. The eye of the camera was really on the Lord Jesus and Judas. This gives us the well-known principle of near and remote fulfillments in connection with the same prophecy, but this is not the case in Psalm

22. Here there is but one individual who walks in the terrible picture. It is none other than the good Shepherd moving into the place of death for His sheep.

Psalm 23 sets the Lord forth in His *present* ministry. Every verb in the psalm is in the present tense. It is something that the Lord Jesus is doing for us *now*. It is the good Shepherd whom we just saw dying in Psalm 22 who is now living as the *great Shepherd* in Psalm 23.

Yes, Psalm 23 presents the Lord Jesus as doing something for me *right now*. In Psalm 22 He did something for me once and forever that He will never have to do again—He died for my sins. But there is something about this old sinful heart of mine that makes it necessary to have Somebody up in heaven to keep it right. Every day and every hour and every moment I have to have Someone living *for* me and *in* me who can crucify every unholy thought, every unholy act, and keep me in a place of usableness before a holy God. And that is exactly what we see Him doing in Psalm 23.

Let us never cease to stand with Paul in the presence of that lone Sufferer on Calvary's cross and say, "He loved *me,* and gave Himself for *me.*" Blessed occupation! But not blessed enough if that is as far as our vision and conception of Calvary extends. Divine urgency is upon us not to engage in this blessed occupation *less,* but to engage in an *additional* occupation which will eventuate in a glorious life of daily victory. Do not *leave* Psalm

22, but do not fail to enter Psalm 23 in daily Christian experience.

It was this progression to new and deeper depths in Christian experience without forsaking the fundamentals and rudiments of that Christian experience which Paul had in mind when he said in Hebrews 6:1-2, "Therefore leaving the principles of the doctrine of Christ, let us go on unto perfection; not laying again the foundation of repentance from dead works, and of faith toward God, of the doctrine of baptisms, and of laying on of hands, and of resurrection of the dead, and of eternal judgment." At first glance this looks like an appeal from Paul for the Christian to *desert* the rudimentary fundamentals and foundations of the Christian faith and go on unto perfection. But a careful examination of the passage discloses that it is exactly the opposite. It is an appeal to go to the perfection of a full, rounded, victorious Christian life based upon these very foundations which he here enumerates.

We see this principle—of progression without forsaking—all around us. The house, in its building, leaves the foundation without forsaking it. The book, in its writing, leaves the alphabet without forsaking it. The anthem leaves the scale without forsaking it. The foundation remains an essential part of the house, but the superstructure is essential also. The alphabet remains a part of the book, but it must be arranged into orderly literature. The scale remains a part of the anthem, but who would want an anthem of all scales and no oratorio? So the Christian, in going on to perfection, leaves some of the first principles without forsaking them. He is not forever to live solely in the glorious realization of sins forgiven through the crucifixion of the good Shepherd. The appeal is to move on from that blessed vantage point into a fuller, richer, deeper, sweeter experience of an increasing knowledge of what the risen Shepherd wants to do for him here and now. This is the story of Psalm 23.

In Psalm 24 we are introduced to the same blessed Person again, but in His ministry as the *chief* Shepherd. The psalmist cries, "Lift up your heads, O ye gates; and be ye lifted up, ye everlasting doors; and the King of glory shall come in. . . . Who is this King of glory? The LORD of hosts, he is the King of glory" (vv. 7-10).

Some expositors have felt that this was the song of the angels welcoming the Lord Jesus back to heaven in the hour of His ascension. But this view does not seem acceptable. The Lord Jesus did not go back to heaven as "the King" and He is not now enjoying the "glory" which shall be His as the King. He went back to heaven not as the *King* but as the *Priest*. Here again we find this same beautiful ministry of Christ represented in the titles Prophet, Priest and King. As the Prophet, He came from God to the people. As the Priest, He went back from the people to God. As the King, He will reign some day. As the Prophet, He told the people the story of God's love in scarlet letters of agony written in the crimson of His own precious blood. This is the story of Psalm 22. As the Priest, He went into the presence of God for His people, there to live for them and in them, and to lead them into the fullness of daily supply. This is the story of Psalm 23. As the King of glory, He will be coming one of these days. What a King He will be and what glory will be His!

It might be of profit for us to examine a little more closely our reasons for rejecting the "welcome" theory to which we have already referred. It seems that the very titles used in the closing verses of Psalm 24 are not those which are applicable to the Lord Jesus in the hour of His ascension, or during the centuries which have passed into history since. He is called in these closing verses, "The King of glory and the Lord of hosts." His prowess on the field of battle is indicated in the title "Lord of hosts." It is true, of course, that the Lord Jesus did engage in a battle on Calvary and in the tomb, but the title here used applies more specifically to His victories in the field of what might be called military conquests. It is the title which pictures Him in furious action and devastating victories in conquest over the kingdoms and schemes of men rather than the great spiritual conquests of Calvary. The demonstration of the Lord Jesus Christ as the Lord of hosts awaits that day when as the King of glory He rides forth on the white steed of heaven to implement His decree which He uttered in Psalm 2 when He declared that He would break the nations "with a rod of iron" and "dash them in pieces like a potter's vessel."

One of these days the Priest will arise from the mercy seat in heaven and will lay aside His priestly robes. His priestly ministry will be over. The two-edged sword will flash from His mouth, fire will leap from His eyes, His feet will become like burnished brass, and upon His thigh will be written the name "King of kings and Lord of lords." As He sits upon the white horse of the skies, poised, ready for the downward rush in all the fury and wrath of God upon a world that has said of Him and His Father, "Let us break their bands asunder and cast away their cords from us," it seems I can see the mighty angel chorus ready at the signal to burst out in mighty song, "Lift up your heads, O ye gates; and be ye lifted up, ye everlasting doors." In other words, roll back the mighty doors and gates of heaven in order that the King of glory, the Lord of hosts, may ride forth in mighty triumph and come into possession of His own kingdom.

Indeed, He will be the King of glory then. That will be the day when the little kings of earth will cry for rocks and mountains to hide them from the wrath of His face. That will be the day when proud, boasting, self-sufficient kingdoms of earth will crumble like dust. That will be the day when every high and haughty imagination of wicked men will burn in the blaze of His fierce anger like a moth caught in the blaze of a blowtorch. That will be the day when even the imaginations of sin will be turned to ashes in the white heat of His holy anger. What a day!

Now it was not a king who went from the tomb to the skies—it was a Priest. There He is to plead His own precious blood on behalf of every trusting soul, there to wash and cleanse every born-again child of God, there to live and lead His people in green pastures and beside still waters. From those same heavens He will come again as the everlasting doors are lifted up. He will come forth as King of glory and Lord of hosts.

The virgin womb opened and gave us the good Shepherd. The virgin tomb opened and gave us the great Shepherd. The virgin skies will open and give us the chief Shepherd.

It is because of all this revelation in Psalm 23 of such abundant blessing and supply for daily, victorious Christian living that we were led to say in the beginning that the psalm sets forth an experience with the Lord Jesus sadly unknown to thousands of born-again believers, *Psalm 23 is the highest, widest, most glorious experience into which it is possible for God to lead a born-again believer this side of heaven.*

Let us look at these triplet psalms (22, 23 and 24) in outline form:

    I. In Psalm 22—Christ forsaken by His Father and despised by the people.

        In Psalm 23—Christ, the living Shepherd.

        In Psalm 24—Christ, the coming King of glory.

    II. In Psalm 22—the cross with its shame.

        In Psalm 23—the crook with its care.

        In Psalm 24—the King with His crown.

    III. In Psalm 22—the *good* Shepherd *in death for* His sheep.

      In Psalm 23—the *great* Shepherd *living for* His sheep.

      In Psalm 24—the *chief* Shepherd *coming for* His sheep.

IV. In Psalm 22—Christ's *yesterday* of suffering.

      In Psalm 23—Christ's *today* of grace.

      In Psalm 24—Christ's *forever* of splendor.

V. In Psalm 22—Christ strengthless.

      In Psalm 23—Christ strengthening.

      In Psalm 24—Christ strong.

VI. In Psalm 22—Christ's cry.

      In Psalm 23—Christ's comfort.

      In Psalm 24—Christ's claim.

VII. In Psalm 22—Christ brought low.

      In Psalm 23—Christ bringing home.

      In Psalm 24—Christ at home.

VIII. In Psalm 22—Christ dishonored.

      In Psalm 23—Christ honoring.

      In Psalm 24—Christ honored.

2

Introduction Continued

BY WAY OF FURTHER INTRODUCTION to the psalm, we now call attention to the fact that the opening verse becomes the theme of the entire psalm. Much, if not most, of the blessed truths set forth in the psalm will be utterly missed unless you take the Shepherd whom you meet in verse 1 with you through the entire psalm. Otherwise the psalm will become just a repetition of "things" which the Shepherd provides. Blessed "things," true, but nevertheless *only* "things" as they are contemplated apart from the Shepherd.

Indeed, it is right here that many Christians miss much in their Christian experience. It is so easy to get into the habit of thinking of our Christian blessing apart from the Blesser—easy but perilous, and well-nigh fatal to the enjoyment of the richest possible Christian experience.

We will have gone a long way in solving the secret of a happy, victorious Christian life when we discover that not a single blessing of the Christian life has any value or significance if divorced from the Person in whom all these blessings are deposited. Preoccupation with the *Person* of Christ is the secret of a life of victory. Preoccupation with the *things* pertaining to the Christian life is too often the cause of discouragement and defeat. It is easily possible for the Sunday school teacher to become so occupied with the technical aspects of her job that she loses almost completely the consciousness of the presence of the one for whom and of whom she is teaching. Many a Bible-class teacher, who at one time was a source of inspiration, comfort and blessing to a Sunday school class, has become just a dry, uninteresting teacher who somehow seems to be isolated from the real need of her pupils. All of this came about because the teacher let the burden of teaching get her down, and she became occupied with the burden instead of the Lord.

Martha of Bethany had to learn this lesson. In Luke 10:38-42, Martha is reported as being greatly out of patience with her sister Mary because she did not help her in the preparation of a little "snack" for not more than four people—herself, her brother Lazarus, her sister Mary, and the Lord. The Lord Jesus rebuked her and told her that she was troubled about "many things" but that Mary had chosen the "better part" (a better thing). There was nothing wrong about getting lunch in that home in Bethany yesterday, and neither will there be tomorrow, but today it was wrong. A thing which is perfectly legitimate today may be out of bounds tomorrow.

One does not have to be engaged in gross worldliness to get out of touch with the Saviour. Perfectly legitimate things can do that to us. The teacher can let her legitimate duties cause her to be fretful and forgetful of Christ. The preacher with the burden of sermon preparation and pastoral duties can do likewise. The church choir can be so occupied with the burden of the music that it is soon singing to an audience which knows that there is something lacking.

Martha accepted her rebuke and instruction, and in John 12 she is getting dinner all by herself again. But this time she prepared for a company which probably numbered twenty-five or thirty, and there is no record of any irritability or short temper. The obvious reason is that she had learned how to carry the presence of the Lord Jesus into the manifold duties of her kitchen. Lunch for four without Him was a burdensome "thing." Dinner for thirty with Him was a joy! Happy the Christian of today who has learned the same lesson!

It is this important point we must keep in mind as we pursue our study of the Twenty-third Psalm. If the sheep tries to find the green pastures and the still waters and the prepared tables and the overflowing cups all by himself, he will have a desperate time which will end only in failure. But if he keeps bringing the Shepherd down into all of these experiences, then the blessings of the psalm are a foregone conclusion.

I once heard Dr. H. O. Van Gilder, commenting on this psalm, say something like this: "If the green pastures in which you have been feeding are suddenly scorched to the roots by the withering sun of adversity, or if the shade tree under which you have been sitting at the side of a wilderness oasis is split from top to bottom by a sudden shaft of lightning, and that which you had hoped to be your shelter for years to come is suddenly laid waste around you, you have a Shepherd who knows where there are other green pastures and other still waters." One thing is certain—when such experiences come to the believer, his eyes are too full of tears to be very successful in finding new pastures and new springs. Happy that believer who, in the midst of all of the disaster which suddenly overtakes him, and when "things" have suddenly vanished, still has with him the blessed consciousness of the presence of the Shepherd. Then he can sing in the words of Sidney Cox's enticing chorus:

My Lord knows the way through the wilderness,
　All I have to do is follow.
My Lord knows the way through the wilderness,
　All I have to do is follow.
Strength for today is mine alway
　And all I need for tomorrow.
My Lord knows the way through the wilderness,
　All I have to do is follow.

The structure of Psalm 23 reminds me of a beautiful rug. Here is a rug made of warp and woof. The woof is the rag which runs crosswise, and the warp is the string which runs lengthwise. This warp is seen on both ends of the rug in the form of fringe, but this visible fringe is simply the extension of the warp which runs the entire length of the rug, and holds the woof, or rags, together in a beautiful pattern. May I reverently liken the Shepherd in this psalm to the warp, and the things into which the Shepherd leads us in this psalm, to the woof? Remember, if you have a rug with no warp and all woof, you may have some beautiful rags but they will be only rags, or just a heap of "things"— beautiful things, but still things. Pick one of them up, and it has no connection with the rest of the pile. But let the long thread of warp run through the woof, over and in and out, over and in and out, and then the rug becomes a complete unit, a perfect whole. The woof is practically useless without the warp.

And thus it is with this blessed psalm. There are so many, many beautiful and wonderful things in this psalm, but only "things" if left detached from each other and isolated from the Shepherd. Keep bringing the "warp" of the presence of the Shepherd right on down through the psalm, in and out, over and in and out again, tying the whole thing together, and making every bit of the woof significant —significant because of its relationship to the warp. We see this blessed "warp" in this psalm showing at both ends of the "rug" in such words as these; "The LORD is my shepherd; I shall not want." And then we drop to the end of the "rug" and find the "warp" showing again: "I will dwell in the house of the LORD for ever." We will miss utterly and ruinously the blessed teaching of this psalm if we fail to keep the warp of the blessed presence of the Shepherd running the entire length of the psalm, and bringing everything into relationship to Himself.

Many years ago I had a Swedish friend named John Linn who loved to work with children. One day while speaking to a Sunday school in the church of a fellow pastor, he asked if there were any children present who could quote the entire Twenty-third Psalm. Among several hands raised was that of a little golden-haired four-and-one-half-year-old girl. My friend was a bit skeptical and asked if she really could quote the entire psalm. Upon being assured that she could, Mr. Linn suggested that she come up to the platform where she could be heard, and repeat the psalm. She came to the rostrum, faced the audience, made a perky little bow, and said, "The Lord is my Shepherd, that's all I want," bowed again, and went and sat down.

Well, she had said it all! That's all there is to the psalm. If the reader can truthfully say today, "The Lord is my Shepherd, that's all I want" then he has compassed the Twenty-third Psalm, for with the Shepherd comes all the rest of the psalm, and without the Shepherd there is very little left.

The little girl was right when she said that if we take the Shepherd out of verse 1 and let Him guide us into all that is offered to us in the rest of the psalm, then we have it all!

Let us not divorce the "things" in the psalm from the Person in whom all these things are deposited. This is discussed further in chapter 9.

Jesus Himself is the believer's attraction. Luke 24:36 reads, "Jesus himself stood in the midst of them." Preoccupation with Christ is the secret of a life of victory.

What Christ *did* in His cross work is the ground of our pardon.

What Christ *is doing* at the Father's right hand is our assurance of security and cleansing.

What Christ *is* in His position and person is the measure of our acceptance and standing.

What Christ *possesses* is the amount of our blessing and property.

What Christ *can be* in us is the cause of our Christlikeness and daily victory.

What Christ *was* in His daily life is the pattern for us to follow.

What Christ *says* is the ground of our faith and the reason for our action.

What Christ *will yet do* is the hope of our expectations.

What He *is* in His image will be the measure of our likeness.

What Christ *is* in Himself is the delight of our love.

3

Rest

WITH THIS QUOTATION of the little girl in mind, we now turn to a detailed exposition of the psalm.

The Lord is my Shepherd; therefore, I shall not want for rest.

"He maketh me to lie down in green pastures" (v. 2).

We are living in a day of extreme weariness. Our minds are tired. Our bodies are tired. Our hearts are tired. Our nerves are tired. Everything about us is tired and exhausted. We live in the constant and ceaseless whirl of things as they are. A thousand eddies in this stream of life seem to catch us every day and whirl us about until we hardly know where we are or why we are there. Strange and mysterious providences crisscross our lives, and one kind of an emotion has hardly risen within our souls before it must give way to another kind. Joy and sorrow. Laughter and tears. Hate and love. Fear and courage. All these seem to be engaged in head-on collisions within this little thing we call "me"; and we are tired enough to drop!

Furthermore, there is no time for us to rest. Everything moves with such lightninglike rapidity. If we should stop and relax a moment, the parade would be so far ahead of us that we would feel we could never catch up. Dr. William L. Pettingill well said, "Our forefathers took months to travel a few miles with an oxcart, but we in this generation cannot even wait for the next section of a revolving door." And how true that is! Three women in our home city were injured by someone in a hurry coming in behind them and literally catapulting them out of a revolving door in one of our large business concerns.

The terrific grind and pressure upon the child of God is by no means lesssening. It is constantly on the increase. Sixty years ago when I went into the ministry it was an easy thing compared to what it is now. Sixty years ago this terrible thing called the apostasy was, to quite an extent, still "underground." It had, of course, manifested itself in many places in the Christian area, but it was far from being as blatant, bold, blasphemous and prevalent as it is today. In those days one met an outright modernist so infrequently that he didn't have to pay too much attention to him. The presence and effect of modernism in our denominational life was not so prevalent and manifest; when it did show itself, there was still plenty of room to move around it.

All of that is now changed. This black, ugly thing called apostasy is now so prevalent and persistent that no Christian minister or layman can dodge it or ignore it for the space of one moment. Modernism, infidelity and compromise have thoroughly entrenched and infiltrated themselves into every phase of Christian living these days. It takes one who is wide awake, reading constantly, and knowing how to evaluate circumstances and analyze situations if he would be his best and his truest for Jesus Christ. The constant mental pressure produced by all of this is terrific. Sometimes I just want to get away somewhere and throw myself into neutral. But I can't. There is no more coasting now. From now on out, it is blood and sweat and tears.

Yes, tired enough to drop. Tired in our souls. Tired in our spirits. Tired in our minds. Tired in our hearts. Tired in our nerves. And no time to rest!

Now, into this situation the Lord Jesus comes and offers Himself to the Christian as a Shepherd who is able to lead every one of His sheep into quiet places where they may lie down and rest. He keeps not only our hearts but also our minds.

There can be no real *rest* without *peace*. One must have peace if he is to rest. This requisite for rest the Shepherd provides, for indeed He Himself is that peace. Ephesians 2:14 says, "For he is our peace."

There are two kinds of peace spoken of in the Scripture. In Romans 5:1 it is "peace *with* God." In Philippians 4:7 it is "the peace *of* God." In these two verses is set before us the very truth we are trying to bring out in this study, and that is that untold thousands of born-again believers who have come to know Christ as their *Saviour* have never yet known Him as their *Shepherd*.

The peace spoken of in Romans 5:1 is the peace which *every* born-again believer has *with* God. The battle is over. The sinner has surrendered and has accepted the peace terms of Calvary. He has received Christ as his only ground of acceptance before a holy God. He now has *peace* about his sins and the consequent guilt. He has peace *with* God.

But in Philippians 4:7 we are to have the peace *of* God, a vastly different thing. The peace of Romans 5:1 *saves the soul*. The peace of Philippians 4:7 *keeps the heart and mind*. It keeps us from worry, fear and unbelief in the loving daily care of a heavenly Father who is too good to be unkind and too wise to make mistakes. It is *this* peace that most born-again believers know little or nothing about and therefore know little or nothing about the green pasture *rest* of Psalm 23. They have met the *Saviour* from sin's guilt in Psalm 22, but how they need to meet Him as the Shepherd of Psalm 23.

The overall picture of the great mass of professing Christians today is appalling. Instead of looking out upon a host of God's own dear ones who "rest in the Lord, and wait patiently for him" (Ps 37:7), we see a crowd of poor, scared, nervous, tired and weary sheep. There is no rest. The flock always seems to be tense. The slightest strange sound, and the sheep become "jittery." The constant bleating of restlessness is heard throughout the flock of God.

The blessed Shepherd is heard to be saying again

and again, "Fear not, little flock" (Lk 12:32), but the sheep are afraid to trust Him and there is no rest.

The Shepherd calls them to *"lie down* in green pastures," but they are afraid to lie down. They must always be ready to run from some expected and feared danger which they are sure the Shepherd can't take care of.

Poor, tired, weary and hungry sheep! How they need to know that the presence of the Shepherd is a guarantee of safety! How they need to know that He is able and sufficient for *any* danger and that if they will but "lie down" and *rest* and eat in peace, He will "work for them that wait for him"! This is the "peace of God" which keeps "heart and mind" in a place of sweet rest from day to day. The peace which He *gives* is in Romans 5:1, but the peace which He *is,* is in Philippians 4:7. If *He* is your Shepherd you "shall not want" for *rest.*

Every farmer knows that a sheep will not lie down and rest if it is hungry. But our text says that if we want "rest" we must "lie down in green pastures." Now, just what *are* these "green pastures"? They are the Word of God given to us in the Bible. Only as we, His sheep, feed in the precious "green pastures" will we know the *peace* which He gives to us and our fears will be calmed and we can really take time to eat. If every believer only knew his Bible! How he would be freed from worry, fearfulness, yielding to temptation and restlessness!

Look for a moment at just what the believer's attitude should be to the Word of God. One great blessing that comes to us is found in Psalm 119:11: "Thy word have I hid in mine heart, that I might not sin against thee." Since the Word of God is able to keep us from sinning against God, how important and necessary it is that our attitude to it be correct! Here are some of those attitudes:

I. We are to receive the Word of God with meekness: "Receive with meekness the engrafted word" (Ja 1:21). Now, just how do we receive it with meekness?

1. As *servants,* for it is the voice of our Master, even the unpleasant duties.

2. As *saints* to cleanse us from defilement (Eph 5:26). Apply the water of the Word to your life when you are conscious of sin—and do it *now*!

3. As *subjects,* for it is the edict of our King.

4. As *soldiers,* for it is the order of our Commander (2 Ti 2:3).

History tells us that Napoleon once called all of his soldiers to stand in review before him. He told them that there was a very important and dangerous commission to be carried out. He informed them that it would take only one man to do it, but that it would mean certain death to the one who undertook it. He said he would turn his back for a moment, and the one who would volunteer should step forward one pace. When he looked again at his army the ranks were unbroken. Not a man was found. One of the soldiers, seeing the grief upon Napoleon's face, said, "Sir, we all stepped forward."

What a day of revival and blessing there would be in this world if *every* child of God would "step forward" to every command of our Commander!

5. As *sons,* for it is our heavenly Father's will. Surely there should be obedience in our heavenly Father's house.

6. As *saved* ones, for it is the voice of the one who took our sins away. What higher, holier motives could there be than to live each day so that when the books for the day are closed at night, there could be only a smile of satisfaction on the face of Christ.

So much for our *attitude* to the Word of God— the green pastures of His supply and peace.

Now here is another approach we must have to the Word of God if we are to "lie down and rest."

II. The Word of God must dwell in us richly (Col 3:16). It must:

1. Dwell in our hearts as a preservation from evil (Ps 119:11).

2. Dwell in our soul as an incentive to service.

3. Dwell in our affections as an anchor to things eternal.

I saw written on the flyleaf of a high school girl's Bible the following words:

> The love of things present is only
> expelled by a clear vision of things
> eternal.   —DOROTHY BURROUGHS

Here is still another approach we must have to the Word of God if we are to "lie down and rest."

III. We must keep God's Word. "They have kept thy word" (Jn 17:6).

1. Keep it as a *treasure*. Suppose we did not have the Bible? We do have it, but do we keep it? We too often treat it as though it did not exist.

2. Keep it as a *trust*. First Peter 4:10 says we are to be "stewards of the manifold grace of God."

IV. We are to continue in the Word of God. "If ye continue in my word, then are ye my disciples indeed" (Jn 8:31).

V. We are to live in the Word of God. "Ye are manifestly declared to be the epistle of Christ . . . written not with ink, but with the Spirit of the living God" (2 Co 3:3).

Has the Spirit been able to write with *your* life?

Our love of the "green pastures" of the Bible will be greatly intensified if we realize that on almost every page of it we will find our lovely Lord waiting for us. Here is where we can find Christ at least once in every book of the Bible:

In Genesis
He is the Creator and Seed of the woman (1:1; 3:15).
In Exodus
He is the Lamb of God for sinners slain (chap. 12).

In Leviticus
  He is our High Priest (entire book).
In Numbers
  He is the Star out of Jacob (24:17).
In Deuteronomy
  He is the Prophet like unto Moses (18:15).
In Joshua
  He is the Captain of the Lord's hosts (5:13-15).
In Judges
  He is the Messenger of Jehovah (3:15-30).
In Ruth
  He is our Kinsman-Redeemer (chap. 3).
In Samuel
  He is the despised and rejected King (I Sa 16-19).
In Kings and Chronicles
  He is the Lord of lords and King of kings (1 Ch 12:38-40).
In Ezra and Nehemiah
  He is the Lord of heaven and earth (entire books).
In Esther
  He is our Mordecai (chap. 10).
In Job
  He is our risen and returning Redeemer (19:25).
In Psalms
  He is the blessed Man of Psalm 1.
  He is the Son of God of Psalm 2.
  He is the Son of man of Psalm 8.
  He is the crucified one of Psalm 22.
  He is the risen one of Psalm 23.
  He is the coming one of Psalm 24.

He is the reigning one of Psalm 72.
He is the Leader of praise of Psalm 150.
In Proverbs
He is our wisdom (chap. 4).
In Ecclesiastes
He is the forgotten wise Man (9:14-15).
In Song of Solomon
He is my Beloved (2:16).
In Isaiah
He is our suffering Substitute (chap. 53).
In Jeremiah
He is the Lord our righteousness (23:6).
In Lamentations
He is the Man of sorrows (1:12-18).
In Ezekiel
He is the one sitting on the throne (1:26).
In Daniel
He is the smiting stone (2:34).
In Hosea
He is David's greater King (3:5).
In Joel
He is the Lord of bounty (2:18-19).
In Amos
He is the Rescuer of Israel (3:12).
In Obadiah
He is the Deliverer upon Mount Zion (v. 17).
In Jonah
He is the buried and risen Saviour (entire book).
In Micah
He is the everlasting God (5:2).
In Nahum
He is our stronghold in the day of wrath (1:7).

In Habakkuk
  He is the anchor of our faith (2:4).
In Zephaniah
  He is in the midst for judgment and cleansing (3:5, 15).
In Haggai
  He is the Lord of presence and power (1:13).
In Zechariah
  He is the smitten Shepherd (13:7).
In Malachi
  He is the sun of righteousness (4:2).
In Matthew
  He is the King of the Jews (2:1).
In Mark
  He is the Servant of Jehovah (entire book).
In Luke
  He is the perfect Son of man (3:38; 4:1-13).
In John
  He is the Son of God (1:1).
In Acts
  He is the ascended Lord (1:8-9).
In Romans
  He is our righteousness (3:22).
In 1 Corinthians
  He is the firstfruits from among the dead (15:20).
In 2 Corinthians
  He is made sin for us (5:21).
In Galatians
  He is the end of the law (3:10; 3:13).
In Ephesians
  He is our armor (6:11-18).

In Philippians
  He is the Supplier of every need (4:19).
In Colossians
  He is the preeminent one (1:18).
In 1 Thessalonians
  He is our returning Lord (4:15-18).
In 2 Thessalonians
  He is the world's returning Judge (1:7-9).
In 1 Timothy
  He is the Mediator (2:5).
In 2 Timothy
  He is the Bestower of crowns (4:8).
In Titus
  He is our great God and Saviour (2:13).
In Philemon
  He is the Father's Partner (vv. 17-19).
In Hebrews
  He is the rest of faith and Fulfiller of types
  (chap. 11; 12:1-2; chap. 9).
In James
  He is the Lord of Sabaoth (5:4).
In 1 Peter
  He is the theme of Old Testament prophecy (1:
  10-11).
In 2 Peter
  He is the long-suffering Saviour (3:9).
In 1 John
  He is the Word of life (1:1).
In 2 John
  He is the target of the Antichrist (v. 7).
In 3 John
  He is the personification of truth (vv. 3-4).

In Jude

He is the believer's security (vv. 24-25).

In Revelation

He is the King of kings and Lord of lords (19: 11-16).

Your Bible will be a new book to you when you learn to discern the outline of His glorious person in the story of other persons and events recorded there.

4

Refreshment

The Lord is my Shepherd; therefore, I shall not want for refreshment.

"He leadeth me beside the still waters" (v. 2).

WE ARE LIVING in a salty old world. How often the salt gets into our eyes and the tears flow like rivers. How often the salt gets into our mouths and leaves us parched and gasping for water! Yea, for fresh water! There was that delightful thing that we were going to partake of, and we were certain that it would be delicious to our taste and satisfying to our hearts. But something happened! Somehow, it didn't turn out that way. Instead, it left our mouths salty and thirsty. It did not satisfy.

There was one thing that our eyes were fastened upon. What a lovely thing! How satisfying to our soul's vision it was going to be. But something happened. It didn't turn out that way. Instead, the salt of bitter disappointment got into our eyes and we cried!

With eyes smarting and throat and lips parched, we sought for refreshing streams. But there were

none. At least *we* couldn't find them. We needed to
be led to them by someone who could.

Now, into this situation the Lord Jesus comes
and offers Himself to the believer as a Shepherd
who knows where there are fresh, living streams of
water in abundance.

Have you been sitting underneath the shade of
some "tree" which you had hoped would shield you
from the hot suns of life, and then suddenly, out of
an apparently blue sky, a bolt of lightning has split
it from top to bottom? Maybe it was your job, and
it was taken from you. Maybe it was your business,
and it failed. Maybe it was your children, and they
have gone. Maybe it was your good health, and
now you are either a partial or total invalid. At any
rate, you are now exposed to the blistering heat of
life as it is.

Have you been feeding in some green pasture and
you felt that it was the *only* green pasture in the
world? If this should be taken away from you, you
would not know what to do. And then suddenly it
was taken away. The hot blistering suns of life
scorched and burned up the grass at its very roots,
and today everything is barren around you.

Have you been drinking at some spring and you
have felt that it was the *only* spring in all the world?
If anything should happen to it, it would be a
tragedy and calamity which could never be overcome. And then suddenly one day the spring wasn't
there, and you stood parched and thirsty. Oh, child
of God, hear the words of our psalm, "I shall not
want"! If the sheltering shade tree has been de-

stroyed, your little green pasture burned up at the roots, and your little spring has become dry as dust, thank God you have a Shepherd who knows where there are other trees, other green pastures, and other fresh fountains. *I shall not want for refreshment.*

Some scholars insist that the word "still" is in the past tense in the original, and that the text should read, "He leadeth me beside the *stilled* waters." Whether or not this is the case, one thing is certain: in the life of the Oriental shepherd he often has to do just that. He must *still* the waters. There is something about a sheep which makes it afraid of swiftly moving water. They seem to have sheep intuition that they are helpless in the water. Their heavy coats act as sponges and become so saturated that the little animals are dragged to the very bottom. Because of this it is difficult, if not well-nigh impossible, to get sheep to go near swiftly running water. It is, however, the business of the shepherd to see to it that his flock is supplied with the refreshment of cool water during the journey on a blistering hot day. If there are no pools or quiet springs, then the shepherd must make some. Just ahead is the swiftly moving little mountain rivulet. Perhaps one could jump across it easily, but the water is dashing so rapidly over the stones that the noise is frightening and the spray is chilling. To such refreshing waters it is impossible for the shepherd to lead his sheep. On occasions like this the shepherd uses rocks and sod from the bank to prepare a little dam across the swiftly moving stream, and by and by there is a quiet little pool of "stilled" waters. The sheep then move forward without fear and are refreshed.

What a beautiful picture of the present ministry of our lovely Shepherd for us who are the sheep of His pasture! Our little stream of life is on a rampage. It is rushing by with a crashing crescendo of frightening noises, the spray of it is dashing into our faces. We cannot see, and we are afraid. Sorrow, affliction, heartache and heartbreak are breaking the speed limit in our lives. Bewilderment and confusion swirl about us like mighty whirlpools. It is then that our blessed Shepherd moves into the situation and "stills" the waters about us, and we discover that through His gracious ministry we are being refreshed by the very thing which would otherwise have been our ruin.

It is a blessed thing indeed to see how the Lord Jesus so often turns these salty and bitter experiences into some of the sweetest and most refreshing experiences of life. That experience through which we have just passed either remains a black and awful memory of fear, bewilderment, confusion and thirst, or it will be remembered as a spot where— in the midst of all of these things—the Lord Jesus Himself became so preciously real that the very waters about us were stilled and we found that we were able to draw actual refreshment for our souls out of the experience. The whole question of whether life's experiences are going to be times of refreshment or ruin is determined by whether or not we constantly recognize the *presence of the Shepherd*. Let us not forget what the little girl said, "The Lord is my

Shepherd, that's all I want." Life will be exceedingly rough and tough for us if we are going it alone, but life may become a thing of beauty if the Shepherd goes along. The Lord Jesus delights to take our troubles and turn them into theaters in which He may display His blessing. Our sin, which could send us to hell, becomes the theater in which the Lord Jesus Christ displays His salvation and, instead, we go to heaven. Our weakness, which would make us powerless and useless, becomes the theater in which the Lord Jesus displays His power and we become instruments of service in His hands.

Many know that I have been afflicted with very poor eyesight throughout my entire ministry. Since the second year of my ministry, in 1913, it has been necessary for me to get print within a half inch of my eyes before I am able to read it. The first nineteen years of my ministry it was necessary for me to memorize all my Scripture, all my hymns, all my pulpit announcements, etc. Then, in 1931, I began using contact lens, which helped my public ministry, but it was still necessary for me to pursue the old close-up method of reading and studying in private. Upon the advice of my doctors a few years ago, I went to New York City where a world-renowned surgeon, Dr. Ramon Castroviejo, performed his famous corneal transplant operation on my right eye. This is an operation where the cornea of the patient's eye is removed, and the cornea from the eye of some dead person is transplanted to the living eye. It is one of the most delicate operations known, and the percentage of success is not great.

The discipline through which the patient must pass is terrible. For eight days and nights he must lie flat upon his back with his head clamped between sandbags so that he cannot move it as much as a fraction of an inch. He is not allowed to yawn, to sneeze, to cough, or to make any other violent or semiviolent muscular movement. He is fed nothing but liquids and very little of them. He lies with both eyes bandaged tightly shut for these eight days and nights. He is kept under powerful opiates and watched ceaselessly by nurses day and night to see that he does not make any sudden move which might ruin the delicate operation.

It was while I was lying thus, flat on my back, in a world of darkness that could be felt, that the dear Lord so often spoke to my troubled heart and brought blessing out of what would otherwise have been complete and total ruin. What would the future hold for me? Would I be able to see again? Or would the operation be a total failure and I would lose what little sight I already possessed? Where were the thousands of dollars to come from to take care of these terrific hospital and doctor bills? If something went wrong with the operated eye, would it react upon the good eye through what is called sympathetic irritation and ruin the one which was not operated upon? Ten thousand questions like these went racing through my mind with express-train speed. Then I would cry out to the Lord and He would so wonderfully and sweetly still the raging waters.

One night I was undergoing one of these times

of testing. As I looked to the Lord for relief and victory, He seemed to speak to me out of the darkness; impressions were left upon my mind that were so precious that I awakened my wife, who was in the hospital room with me, and asked her to write them down before they escaped me. Here they are, just as I dictated them to my wife at 3 A.M. in the New York City hospital:

> These days we need to know the secret of being occupied only with Him and not with "things." Martha got into trouble worrying about "things." Mary got into blessing by being occupied with Him. As a *faithful* Shepherd our Lord *must* lead us into the *shadows* as well as into the *sunshine*. It is how *we* react that makes the difference between defeat and victory. If we become preoccupied with the *shadows,* we will become cynical, bitter, discouraged and defeated. If we become *preoccupied* with the *sunshine,* we will become self-satisfied, self-centered, thoughtless of others, and worse still, forgetful of *Him.* But if we remain *preoccupied* with the *Shepherd,* regardless of shadow *or* sunshine, we will survive *the peril of both* with victory!

Thus it was that I had another experience of seeing the Shepherd still the waters and take the very experiences which threatened and turn them into pools of quiet refreshment.

In September, 1932, I became pastor of the Central Baptist Church of Gary, Indiana. The following May I was to address a gathering in the First Baptist Church of Buffalo, New York. As I stepped to the pulpit to begin my message, an usher handed me a telegram from my wife. It read as follows: "BABY EVANS KILLED TODAY. FUNERAL FRIDAY." Naturally the eyes of hundreds were upon me, and it was incumbent upon me to advise them of the nature of the telegram.

As I looked out over the crowded auditorium, I spoke in the following manner: "I do not know how the Evans baby was killed. Apparently it has been a tragic accident of some kind. But one thing I do know, beloved, is that there is a little Welsh mother in Gary, Indiana, tonight who is riding out the storm. I have been her pastor for only about nine months but I have been her pastor long enough to know that Mrs. Evans is not abandoning herself to screaming hysteria in this dark hour, but rather to a calm and quiet resting upon the sweet will of God."

Friday morning my wife met me at the train and, of course, my first question was as to what had happened. I was informed that the baby had been struck and instantly killed by a speeding South Shore Interurban electric train. The Evanses lived only three doors away from the tracks where, at this point, the passenger electric trains traveled at a speed of from seventy to eighty miles an hour. Naturally every precaution was taken to watch that the baby did not get near these tracks. The family had just finished supper. The little two-year-old, golden-haired baby girl had gotten down from her high chair. Not more than five minutes had elapsed when they suddenly missed her. Failing to find her in the house, they went to the door to look outside.

As they reached the door, the men were bringing the mangled little body up the front steps. She had been struck by a speeding train.

My wife then went on to tell me of how graciously the Lord was manifesting Himself to Mrs. Evans in this sad hour. Many scores of people had gone to the Evans' home to express their sympathy, but somehow they had all gone away feeling that they were the ones who had been comforted. My wife said she herself had gone to the home to offer sympathy and have prayer with the stricken mother. But before she could get a chance to express the feeling of of her own heart, Mrs. Evans was gripping her hand, and through the tears, with a smile upon her face, was giving testimony as to how wonderful it was to know the Saviour in an hour like this. How glad she was to know that she had a heavenly Father too good to be unkind, and too wise to make mistakes, and that He certainly was one who did all things well.

Several months later the motorman who was driving the train the day of the tragedy came to the Evans' home to offer apologies and explanations. Mrs. Evans, instead of discussing the tragedy, asked if he were a Christian. She told him how she, as the mother of the little girl, would never have been able to carry through had it not been for the comforting presence of the dear Lord, and how she had so often prayed that he too might become a Christian so that he could have the same comforting help in the hour of what must have been his mental anguish. So eloquently did she witness to him of Christ, and not only of His saving but of His keeping power, that later the man became a Christian. The last I heard, he was walking daily with the Saviour.

That is what we mean when we say with the little girl, "The Lord is my Shepherd, that's all that I want." He leadeth me beside the *stilled* waters, and I shall not want for *refreshment*.

5

Restoration

The Lord is my Shepherd; therefore, I shall not want for restoration.

"He restoreth my soul" (v. 3).

HERE THE PICTURE of the Oriental shepherd beautifully illustrates the spiritual truth of the psalm. Often the shepherd will be bothered with one or two sheep in the flock which insist upon straying. The sheep gets its head down into a juicy tuft of grass and from there moves to another and yet another and never looks up to see where the shepherd and the flock might be.

Suddenly it raises its head only to discover that the shepherd and the flock are nowhere in sight. There it stands alone and afraid. But over the brow of yonder knoll comes the faithful shepherd and leads it back to the flock. The sheep is restored.

Sometimes the sheep gets the miserable habit of straying thus from the flock, and it is always the business of the shepherd to restore it. However, he has two ways of accomplishing this. One is the gentle process just described. But if the sheep in-

sists upon straying time after time and will not stay
close to the shepherd and to the flock, then more
drastic measures must be used.

One day the shepherd comes over the hilltop and
instead of gently and patiently leading the wayward
sheep back to the flock, he reaches down and takes
one of the slender front legs in his hand and strikes
it a sudden blow with the shepherd's crook and
there is a sheep with a broken leg. Broken by the
shepherd! He then prepares splints and binds up the
broken leg. Thereafter, the wounded sheep must
of necessity keep close to the shepherd for he must
carry it over rough spots and across the mountain
streams. But the point is, the shepherd has restored
the sheep.

Here again the Lord Jesus Christ is our faithful
Shepherd, and because He is "I shall not want for
restoration." He will restore our souls. How tempt-
ing the tufts of green grass seem to us sometimes!
We get our hearts set upon something we want, and
that in turn leads to something else we want, and
from there on to still something more we want, until one day we pause a moment to discover that we
have not only estranged ourselves from the flock of
God, but we have lost the conscious presence of the
Shepherd. Then it is we stand alone and afraid. But,
blessed be God, then it is, too, that the Shepherd
restores our soul by His infinite mercy. Sometimes
He succeeds in doing this by His work of chastening. Many a hospital bed, automobile wreck, lost
job, ruined business, or bereaved life has been the
"broken leg" method by which the Shepherd re-

stores the soul. But in either case, whether it be by patience or by chastening, it is mercy—boundless, endless, infinite mercy.

We need to pause here long enough to point out that it is not always the sheep's nibbling in "wild" grass which gets it into trouble, but more frequently it is its persistent nibbling in "good" grass which results in a conscious separation from the presence of the shepherd. It is true that many of God's children find themselves out of fellowship with the Shepherd by reason of worldliness or "wild" grass in their lives. But it is our observation that far more of them are living in a place where they do not realize the blessed presence of the Shepherd because of their occupation with and concentration upon actually good things. To most born-again Christians, worldliness itself is a sufficient warning that it is out of bounds, but the deadly thing which I have seen working in the lives of countless thousands of God's people is their apparent, almost total, unawareness of the fact that perfectly good and legitimate things can separate them from the conscious presence of the Shepherd just about as effectually as do the things of the world.

This principle was pointed out in an earlier chapter, but it is of sufficient importance to reiterate it here. The pastor may become busy with sermon preparation, pastoral calling and a thousand other things, all of them good in themselves. But if they become the dominant things in his life, he will find himself altogether too frequently "on the other side of the knoll," and will have to know the experience of the Shepherd's coming to him, either gently or otherwise, and bringing him back into fellowship with Himself. Preoccupation with "things," even good things, may become disastrous. Fellowship with the Shepherd is victory.

Many a deacon has found himself eventually out of fellowship with the Lord because he has become overburdened with the duties of his office. And so with many a trustee, Sunday school teacher, choir singer, young people's worker and other Christian workers.

It is this thing which I referred to in an earlier chapter when I called attention to Martha's experience. She was all upset and distraught with the burden of getting a noonday snack for four people. When she complained to the Lord about her sister's indolence in the matter, the Lord rebuked her by calling her attention to the fact that she was worried about many "things," but that Mary had chosen the better part.

Certainly there was nothing wrong in getting lunch. It was a perfectly legitimate thing to do. But it was not the perfectly legitimate thing to do *on that occasion*. It was all right yesterday, and it will be all right again tomorrow to get lunch, but this day lunch was out of bounds for Martha. It is this principle which we as God's born-again people need to get clearly in mind: things which may be perfectly legitimate for us today may be out of bounds for us tomorrow. This makes it necessary for a constant realization of daily, hourly, moment-by-moment conscious guidance by the Shepherd.

Where is the Shepherd taking me *today?* What does He want me to do *today? Where am I to feed with Him today?* The very grass that I fed upon yesterday and will feed upon again tomorrow may be out of the Lord's diet for me *today.* I can become so occupied with the good things, multiplied by things until they mount up around me, and I keep on nibbling here and nibbling there until suddenly I stop to breathe, then I find I've lost the sweet touch of the Shepherd's presence and have gotten myself out of fellowship with some of the sheep.

However, we must not overlook the fact that many Christians do get away from the Shepherd by eating "wild grass." They go far from Him by disobeying His command to "have no fellowship with the unfruitful works of darkness" (Eph 5:11).

Many illustrations are recorded in the Bible of such wandering away from the Shepherd (1 Ki 3:1; chaps. 9, 11). Against God's command that Jews should not marry outside their own nation, 1 Kings 7:8 records that Solomon had married one of Pharaoh's daughters and that he "made affinity" with Pharaoh. It was from this land that God had *redeemed* and *separated* Israel by blood and by power. Solomon's act was a repudiation of this separation.

We have been redeemed and separated from the world by the blood of the cross. "Who gave himself for our sins, that he might deliver us from this present evil world" (Gal 1:4). Again in Galatians 6:14, "But God forbid that I should glory, save in the cross of our Lord Jesus Christ, by whom the world is crucified unto me, and I unto the world." To overstep this separation is to ignore and repudiate the cross which made the separation.

We need to remember that when we go into the world, we always bring some of that world back to live with us (1 Ki 9:24). What a sad thing to go into a home which is professedly Christian and find the world installed there. The home, regulated by the principles of the world, is full of the art, fashion, philosophy and conversation of the world—a home where Christ is merely an incident and the world an abiding fact.

We need to take account of what Isaiah said to King Hezekiah in Isaiah 39:1-4. The son of the king of Babylon sent gifts to Hezekiah and then came with others to visit him. Hezekiah showed them every lovely thing he had in his house, but he did not set before them the glory of the Lord. Not once did he speak of the Lord's redeeming love and grace. Instead he showed them the things of the world. Isaiah rebuked the king and said, "What have they seen in thine house?" Let every Christian answer! What does the world see in your house?

In 1 Kings 9—11 we see the terrible wreck. It was the ignoring of the doctrine of separation on the part of Solomon that brought this wreckage. It is the ignoring of this same doctrine by Christians that is bringing wreck and ruin to the influence of the professing church today.

If you are away from the *presence* of the Shepherd, get back to Him now. Whether it was "good grass" or "wild grass" that left you estranged from your lovely Shepherd, do something about getting back into fellowship with Him now.

6

Guidance

The Lord is my Shepherd; therefore, I shall not want for guidance.

"He leadeth me in the paths of righteousness" (v. 3).

WE ARE LONELY TRAVELERS across this great expanse of wilderness called life. Ten thousand voices and as many different paths are constantly beckoning us to go this way and that. For the most part, we wander on in bewilderment, slipping into the first path which for the moment looks good to us. When we find that it ends in rocks and thorns, we desperately try another one. "If I only knew what to do" is the most common expression wrung from human lips. Life to most folks is like a road map of the United States without the name of a town or the number of a route—just roads and roads and roads. Which one we are on, which one we want, and where we are, are all bothersome uncertainties. Seeking to find our way through this labyrinth of crisscross highways and bypaths leaves us bewildered and confused and even desperate.

Now into this situation comes the Lord Jesus as

our Shepherd and offers Himself to the child of
God as the Guide who will lead in paths of righteousness, or paths that are right. Divine guidance
is not some sentimental theory. Divine guidance is
a blessed reality.

Any child of God who is willing to meet the
scriptural requirements necessary to guidance may
know with absolute certainty the path to take. He
will hear behind him a voice saying, "This is the
way. Walk ye in it and turn not, neither to the right
nor to the left, for then shall ye go into paths which
shall neither profit nor deliver."

Someone asks, "How do I know whether it is the
Lord speaking to me or someone else?" We could
give many answers to that question, chief among
which would be that familiarity with a voice is a
pretty sure safeguard against following a strange
voice. But why should we labor to answer this
question when in John 10:4b-5 the Lord Jesus
Himself answers it when He says, "The sheep follow him: for they know his voice. And a stranger
will they not follow . . . for they know not the voice
of strangers." Yes, divine guidance is one of the
surest, sweetest realities in Christian experience.

Perhaps we should pause here and linger a while
as we discuss this matter of guidance. In Colossians
1 is a wonderful revelation of not only the possibility of knowing the will of God for our lives, but
what will happen in the life of a Christian who
knows and does the will of God. In verses 9 to 12
are these wonderful words: "For this cause we also,
since the day we heard it, do not cease to pray for

you, and to desire that ye might be filled with the
knowledge of his will in all wisdom and spiritual
understanding; that ye might walk worthy of the
Lord unto all pleasing, being fruitful in every good
work, and increasing in the knowledge of God;
strengthened with all might, according to his glorious power, unto all patience and longsuffering with
joyfulness; giving thanks unto the Father, which
hath made us meet to be partakers of the inheritance of the saints in light."

Paul is here praying that the Colossian church
might be filled with the knowledge of God's will.
Certainly he would not have prayed thus if it had
not been possible for these Colossian Christians to
be so filled.

We hear Paul expressing the same conviction in
Ephesians 1:18 where he declares, "The eyes of
your understanding being enlightened; that ye may
know what is the hope of his calling, and what the
riches of the glory of his inheritance in the saints."
The "hope of his calling" here referred to is not, in
our opinion, the Christian's hope of salvation which
is realized in Christ. In this verse it is rather Christ's
hope from the life of His redeemed one. In other
words, it is what *Christ* hoped for when He saved
you that is here referred to. Jesus Christ invested
Himself in the purchase of every believer on Calvary's cross. He has a definite plan and purpose for
every one of those believers. He hopes for a definite
return on that investment from every life thus redeemed. Paul is here suggesting that every believer
ought to explore the mind of God to find out what

it is that Jesus Christ expects to secure from His investment in this particular life so that Christ's "inheritance in the saints" may not be frustrated. It is simply saying in another way what Paul says in Colossians, that he desires that every Christian shall be filled with the knowledge of God's will.

It is important to notice, furthermore, in the Colossian passage that Paul qualifies the knowing of God's will by suggesting that it should be "in all wisdom and spiritual understanding." It is not enough to know the will of God for one's life. It is equally important to know how to accomplish that will, or how to do what God wants done. Many a child of God has utterly ruined his life by doing the will of God for his life in an utterly wrong fashion.

We have a biblical illustration of this principle in the case of Moses. If ever there was a man who knew what God's will for his life was, it was Moses. He knew it so strongly that it pulled him out of the palace, where he could have been prime minister of the greatest nation on earth, to become identified with a downtrodden slave race. He knew it was God's will for him to turn his back upon Egypt and engage in the deliverance of the Jewish people. With this knowledge of God's will in his mind, he moved out of the palace and proceeded to go about the prescribed task. But how wretchedly he went about it! He finished off one Egyptian and buried him under the sand, not realizing that if that was the way he was to accomplish the deliverance of Israel he wouldn't live long enough to get all the Egyptians killed one at a time, and there wouldn't be sand enough in Egypt to cover them if he did. Here was a man who knew what God's will for his life *was,* but he didn't know *how* to go about it. The Lord graciously took him to the back side of the desert and put him in school for forty years; and when he had learned how to go about the business of doing the will of God in God's way, he was sent back and the mighty deliverance of Israel was accomplished.

It was alone with God on the back side of the desert that Moses learned a lot of things about God, as well as learning how to do His will. "Now Moses kept the flock of Jethro his father in law, the priest of Midian: and he led the flock to the backside of the desert, and came to the mountain of God, even to Horeb" (Ex 3:1).

It is there and then that we too may learn about Him. When He calls us to come aside and spend some time alone with Him then He can make us realize just how precious and wonderful He is. There, alone with God on "the backside of the desert," the enemy of your soul cannot gild the sands of that spot!

There, alone with God, the din and confusion of the world do not fall upon your ear in that distant place.

There, alone with God, the crash in the money and commercial world is not heard.

There, alone with God, the sigh of ambition is not heard.

There, alone with God, the world's laurels do not tempt.

There, alone with God, the thirst for gold is not felt.

There, alone with God, the eye is never dimmed with lust.

There, alone with God, the heart is never swollen with pride.

There, alone with God, human applause does not elate.

There, alone with God, human censure does not depress.

There, alone with God, nothing is seen or heard except the stillness and light of God's presence.

Would to God that all of us would know more about "the backside of the desert" of an aloneness with God!

Alone with God is the place of searching for the guidance of God, and the place of committal to it.

The experience of the "backside of the desert" of an aloneness with God may mean for you what Isaiah meant. When speaking of Christ's ministry to us he said, "To give unto them beauty for ashes, the oil of joy for mourning, the garment of praise for the spirit of heaviness; that they might be called trees of righteousness, the planting of the LORD, that *he* might be glorified" (Is 61:3).

Considering further our little side trip into Colossians under the subject of guidance, we would point out that there are seven direct results enumerated by Paul which will be found in the life of every individual, and in the collective life of every church, where the will of God is known and done in God's way. Paul prays that these Colossian Christians may be filled with the knowledge of God's will *in order that* they may walk worthy of the Lord unto all pleasing (in all things to please God), that they may be fruitful unto every good work, that they may increase in the knowledge of God, that they might be strengthened with all might according to His glorious power, that they might have all patience in longsuffering, that they might be joyful, and furthermore, that they might give thanks unto the Father. Here, then, are seven things which will characterize the life of every person who knows and does the will of God in God's way. He will be obedient, fruitful, growing, strengthened, patient, joyful and thankful.

But someone says that it is utterly impossible for the finite to explore the mind of the Infinite to know beyond a shadow of a doubt what God's will is for one's life. They say that the best you can do is to do the best you can, and you will never know whether you have hit it or missed it until you get to heaven. They insist that there is a vast amount of Christian work to do, and everyone should pitch in and get it done. But that each individual worker should apply to the Lord for instructions as to *where* to work and *how* to work in this field of vast Christian service never enters their heads; and if it does, it is immediately dismissed as being an impossible proposition. The result is confusion, failure, discouragement and disheartenment all through the church of Jesus Christ. It ought not so to be, and it does not need to be so.

If, as an earthly father, I can tell my son what it

is I want *him* to do in my house today, and how and when I want it done, then shall we insist that our heavenly Father is any less capable of making His will known to His children who desire to be obedient to Him? We *can* know God's will if we *want* to know it. We can know God's will if we want to know it *in order to do it*. If we want to know God's will in order to take it under advisement and vote on it, we are not in a very enviable position in relation to knowing His will. We can know God's will if we want to know it in order to do it *because we love it*—and this last observation is the crux of the matter. Do we *love* to do God's will more than we love anything else on earth? Do we get more downright delight and pleasure out of obeying God than we do out of anything else? Would we rather find God's way and walk in it than to think even of considering our own way and walking in it? If this is our *heart attitude* toward the will of God, we may rest assured that God stands ready to reveal His will and give complete and perfect guidance to such a trusting, obedient and loving heart.

Dorothy Burroughs was a freshman in the Gary, Indiana, high school. Her father, one of the high officials in the Gary steel mills, was not a Christian. Her mother was a very worldly professing Christian.

One Sunday morning Dorothy confessed Christ as her Saviour. In all my ministry I never saw any young convert develop in the knowledge of Christ and the Bible as rapidly as Dorothy. She really ate the Word.

Dorothy was a gifted and talented girl in all of the cultural graces. She was outstanding in music, both vocal and instrumental, and excelled in prose, poetry and elocution. She was determined that she and all her talents should be given to her Lord in a life of service. Her aim was the foreign mission field.

In her sophomore year she was stricken with what was called in those days "quick consumption." In a few months she was dead.

I knew that she made notes in her Bible. I asked her mother if I could use Dorothy's Bible in my preparation for her funeral service. As I leafed through it I noticed that she put my initials beside the text of my sermons and the date of delivery.

When I came to Colossians I found her note on a sermon I had preached one Sunday morning on Colossians 1:9-12. My outline was:

I. You can know the will of God if you want to.

II. You can know the will of God if you want to know it to do it, not to vote on it.

III. You can know the will of God if you want to know it to do it because you love it.

She had written these words on the margin: Know, Do, Love.

In her Bible there was nearly a whole page at the end of Colossians. In the blank space she had written this magnificent poem:

I asked the Lord for some motto sweet,
Some rule of life with which to guide my feet.
I asked, and paused. He answered soft and low,
"God's will to know."

"Will knowledge then suffice, dear Lord?" I cried.
But 'ere the question into silence died—
"Nay, this remember, too.
God's will to do."

Once more I asked, "Is there no more to tell?"
And once again the answer sweetly fell,
"Yes, this one thing—all other things above—
God's will to love."

On the back flyleaf of her Bible she had written another poem which was dated just three days before she died:

God let me lose triumphantly,
This is my prayer today.
I, who had always prayed to win
Along a glorious way.
God let me shun all bitterness
Of envy or despair.
That I have run the race and lost,
While others have gotten there.
God let me get my breath again
Then, Lord, my head still high.
Quite unashamed I did not win
Proud I had dared to try.

Poems like these could only come from a heart that knew that *both* sunshine and shadow come from the hand of a heavenly Father who is too good to be unkind and too wise to make mistakes. Sixteen high school students were saved the day of her funeral.

7

Courage

The Lord is my Shepherd; therefore, I shall not want for courage.

"I will fear no evil: for thou art with me" (v. 4).

IF THERE IS ONE THING above another that a sheep needs, it is courage—but not courage to fight. A sheep cannot fight. She has nothing to fight with. In fact, she is about the most helpless animal in the domestic world. Why, then, does the sheep need courage? It could have all the courage of a lion and still be utterly helpless in the face of a little sheep-killing dog. The sheep needs courage, not to fight the lion, but to *trust the shepherd*. And we may say to you most emphatically that it takes more courage to trust the Shepherd than it does to fight the lion.

If we only have a sense of "doing something" to defend ourselves; if we can only feel that we, in our own strength, have delivered a knockout blow to Satan at some point in our life, how good we feel! But we have nothing within ourselves with which to deliver knockout blows to Satan. We are not equipped with a single solitary thing with which to fight; we are just helpless sheep. And unless the Shepherd can take care of the enemies, we are sure to be found somewhere on the desert of life torn and bleeding.

Now, into this situation comes the Lord Jesus Christ and offers Himself to every believer as a Shepherd who is sufficient for every emergency and danger of life.

When the flock is feeding and a sheep has its nose down in a tender juicy tuft of grass and it hears the roar of the lion as it comes pouncing down out of the mountainside, all the sheep needs to do is to lift its head to make sure that the shepherd is standing close by; then put its nose back into the green tuft of grass and continue eating, leaving the lion to the shepherd. And that takes courage!

How often we allow the frightening things of life to interrupt our feeding in the green pastures! We get so afraid, and we roll up our sleeves and square off for action. Don't do it! You are whipped before you begin. Go ahead and eat and drink and let the Shepherd do the fighting.

I once saw a wonderful demonstration of this kind of trusting when the enemy attacks. I was visiting my son, Donn Ketcham, a medical doctor serving the Lord as a missionary in East Pakistan (now Bangladesh). One of the converts from Islam was a young man named Syeed.

When Syeed was first converted (about a year before we were there) he was beaten nearly to death by the Muslims in his little village which was located about three miles from the hospital where my son serves. He was then taken to a little island in the Bay of Bengal and left to die. But he recovered and somehow made his way back to the hospital.

When we arrived there the Bible school was in progress. Missionary Jay Walsh was teaching a class of about thirty newly saved Muslims. Among them was Syeed.

Mr. Walsh asked me to teach for three mornings while he interpreted. I used Psalm 23 for my lessons. One morning someone came in and took Syeed out. In about five minutes he came back in and sat down. I was just discussing verse 4, "I will fear no evil." I was emphasizing that when wild men and evil things come upon us, we should first take a look to see if the Shepherd is near; then we should put our little old sheep nose back in the grass and leave the evil men and evil things to Him.

As I said this, a strange thing happened. Syeed looked at me with staring eyes. Suddenly he lifted his head and cried out the only English word he knew, "Hallelujah!" Rivers of tears rolled down his cheeks, and his face shone with the very glory of God.

When the class was over we found out what all this emotion was about. Seven Muslim men had come onto the hospital grounds and asked some of the workmen to bring Syeed to them. One of them came and called him out. These men said to him, "You cannot be a Christian. You are a Muslim." He said, "I am a Christian." They said, "You say you are a Muslim or we will kill you now." Once more Syeed said, "I am a Christian and I will go with my Bible." The Lord then took over!

The men silently slunk away, and Syeed came back in just in time to hear me say, "Keep your nose in the Book and leave the evil men to the Lord." *Syeed had just come from doing that very thing and it worked.* The glory of the whole experience was that Syeed had done just what I was teaching *but he did it before he heard me say it!*

Several years ago when former President Roosevelt came back from the North Atlantic Conference, he announced that they had made plans on board this great battleship for the elimination of the "four fears" and that they had also instituted a program on the positive side which was to be called the "four freedoms." The idea was that there were to be four freedoms to offset the four fears. Well, since then, we have witnessed a spectacle—not the elimination of the four fears, but the multiplication of those fears into forty-four and more! The freedoms which were promised by Mr. Roosevelt and his colleagues are somewhere "just around the corner," but I am terribly afraid that the corner is so infinitely removed from us that there's no use of our expecting to turn it in our lifetime!

As we turn away in utter disgust from the programs of man which are designed to bring the kingdom of God on earth with all of its consequent blessing to humanity, we turn in expectation to the Son of God Himself. He brings us infinite reassurance that what man cannot do, God can and will do.

So consider the fact that we may now, as believing children of the Lord, have soul peace and freedom from fear in the midst of a world that is thoroughly messed up by the human endeavors of novices.

The world is full of fear. As I travel this continent, I find almost every person with whom I come in contact more or less actuated by fear. In Pullman trains, buses, hotel lobbies, dining cars, barber shops—in fact, wherever one comes in contact with men—this terrible sense of fear pervades the whole atmosphere. Men are afraid of what is coming tomorrow. If Job had been a modern newspaper columnist, he could not have closed his article for today with any more appropriate and descriptive words than he used when he closed chapter 12 of the book which bears his name. The last two verses of that chapter read as follows:

> He taketh away the heart of the chief of the people of the earth, and causeth them to wander in a wilderness where there is no way.
> They grope in the dark without light, and he maketh them to stagger like a drunken man.

Indeed it is a poor, blind, staggering, fear-ridden world which we live in today, and well it might be for those who know not the Lord Jesus Christ in all of His power to impart a courage and a peace that passeth understanding.

The tragedy of this terrible orgy of fear, however, is that it has swallowed up a lot of Christians and they too are fearful of what tomorrow will bring forth. It is to such that I address myself now.

In Revelation 1:17-18, the risen Saviour says, "Fear not; I am the first and the last: I am he that liveth, and was dead; and, behold I am alive for evermore, Amen; and have the keys of hell and of death."

In John 6:20 are the Saviour's reassuring words to the storm-tossed disciples on the Sea of Galilee: "It is I; be not afraid."

If we are Christians we not only belong *to* Christ, but according to the Scriptures, God views us as actually being *in* Christ. When Christ died, we died; when Christ arose, we arose; when Christ ascended, we ascended; where Christ goes, we go. If this is not true, then what does the Scripture mean when in Romans 6 it declares that we are crucified with Christ, and in Ephesians 2:6 where it declares that we are raised together and seated together with Christ, and again in Colossians 3:4 where it declares that when Christ appears we shall appear with Him?

Why should our hearts be filled with fear? Christ is not only the first, but He is the last. He was not only "before all things" but He will be here when all things as we know them now will have passed away; and if we are *in* Christ, then we too will survive the ordeal of existence.

Vance Havner well says, "He [God] was here before there was any fear and He will be here when all fear has passed away. Let us remember that He saw everything before there was anything. If we could stand at His side today and see what He sees, how baseless would be our fears and how excuseless our tears! But we cannot see *as* He sees, nor can we see *what* He sees. Our vision of the future does not extend beyond our faces so far as certainty is concerned. We live in the mixed and muddled present."

We look at the tapestry of our life with its beautiful pattern of variegated colors, and there is a particular spot which is woven in deep crimson. It was there that we suffered so terribly. We reach out and tear that crimson spot out of the whole beautiful fabric and say, "This is life. It is hard. It is cruel. It is unfair." But wait. Put that crimson piece back into the tapestry and stand off and view it in its relationship to the golds and the purples and the blues which surround it, and you will discover that it required just that crimson spot in your life to complete the beauty in the pattern. Without it the whole pattern would have been flat. So often we tear one page out of the book of our life—that page which was written in scarlet letters of awful agony—and we say, "This is life." No, put the page back into the book and read the whole book—begin with babyhood, read on through childhood, youth, young womanhood, young manhood, on down through the sunset days of old age—and you will discover that the book would have been terribly dull were it not for such pages. Our trouble is that we forget the blues and the golds already woven into the pattern, and the pages of pleasure already written into the book, and, since we cannot see what the future is to produce, we get terribly afraid as we view the awful present. But remember that you are in the one who sees it all and, seeing to the end, He turns to you and whispers, "Fear not."

If we could see what He sees, if we could see ourselves arriving with Him and in Him at the destination of eternity, then our fears would be allayed. No, we cannot see what He sees, but I'll tell you what we can do: we can hear what He says; and in spite of all the tragedy and suffering which His omniscient eye detects as coming into our life in the days ahead, He sees with that same omniscient eye our safe arrival in eternity. So, cannot we trust Him even though we cannot see? If by some means you could be made absolutely certain that you were going to arrive safely and without harm at a certain destination, would not that assurance and guarantee in itself be sufficient to allay any fear which might be occasioned by a bit of rough going enroute? The one who not only sees the end from the beginning, but who also maps out the course and does the driving, whispers in your ear today, "I am the first. I am the last. I was dead. I am alive. I know all the way, and I know the end of the way, and I am saying to you today, 'Fear not.' "

To the fearful sinner, He says, "Be not afraid; I am thy Saviour." To the one who is afraid of losing his way, He says, "Fear not, I am the way." To the one who is afraid of death, He says, "Be not afraid, I am the resurrection and the life." To the one who is afraid of hell, He says, "Be not afraid, I am He that hath the keys of hell." It is this Saviour who is waiting today to come into your life and say,

"Peace be unto you; my peace I leave with you. I am the first and I am the last. Fear not."

Sophie, a scrubwoman, was a poor, little old lady who made her living cleaning offices. But she was known by countless thousands all over the world as one of God's choice children. There was hardly a fundamental mission station in the world that she was not familiar with and knew all about their needs. Many wealthy Christian men, knowing Sophie's knowledge of these mission stations, would send her thousands of dollars and tell her to forward it to the mission field where it was most needed.

It was a great blessing to know Sophie and to see her trust the Lord daily for all her needs. One day Dr. W. W. Rugh and I were walking down a street in Philadelphia with Sophie. As she walked ahead of us, every time she raised her foot from the sidewalk we could see bare skin showing through the sole of her shoe. Brother Rugh said, "Sophie, you need a new pair of shoes." Sophie stopped, looked up toward heaven, and said, "Father, Brother Rugh says I need a new pair of shoes. Will You please take care of that?" We then went on down the street. The next day Sophie showed up with a new pair of shoes. Where did she get them? We asked her and her reply was, "Didn't you hear me ask my Father for them yesterday?"

In 1919, Dr. W. B. Riley and others of us under his leadership started a worldwide, fundamentalist Bible conference. Its first session was held in the Academy of Music hall in Philadelphia.

One of the speakers was Dr. William Evans. Dr. Evans was not only one of the world's greatest preachers, but he was also an excellent orator. His message was about our wonderful Lord as He is described in Revelation 1:8: "I am Alpha and Omega, the beginning and the ending." At one point in his message he put all of his oratorial gifts into his voice and cried, "I am Alpha and Omega, the beginning and the ending." He then paused for oratorial effect and every one of the 3,000 people was sitting on the edge of his seat. You could have heard a pin drop!

Sophie was sitting in the middle of the front row in the balcony. Suddenly the silence was broken when she cried out in her high voice, "Yes, Dr. Evans, and He is everything in between, too!"

Is Christ your Shepherd the *beginning* and the *end* and everything in between to you?

Before we move deeper into verse 4 of this psalm, think about this word "shadows." It is called "the valley of the shadow of death." Whose death? It is the shadow of *His* death.

That shadow is upon everything about us. When He came down from heaven to earth, the world gave Him a cross. The political world gave Him a cross. The social world gave Him a cross. The educational world gave Him a cross. The religious world gave Him a cross.

Our Christ came and this is what the world gave Him. There He is—thorn-crowned, blood-soaked, spit-bedraggled, nailed fast to the accursed tree! He is put there by a combination of all phases of human life. That cross was the *total* gift to our Lord by a *total* world.

Thus it is today. All that the world says or does throws a shadow—the shadow of *His* death.

It was this world who murdered the one who loved you so that He went to that murderous cross for you. An illustration will bring the awfulness of this "shadow" into fuller view. You are standing in an art gallery, looking at and admiring a beautiful painting. As you stand there, someone walks up to you and says, "Are you the lady whose fiancé was murdered last week?" You reply, "Yes, I am." The person tells you that the man who painted that picture is the man who murdered your lover. Then, suddenly, every line in that picture is turned into shadowy, horrid and awful lines. The shadow of the man who killed your lover has changed it all.

So, let us look at this Christ-rejecting world that killed our lovely Lord. As we look at it through the shadow of His death it will surely put to death our love for the world.

8

Comfort

The Lord is my Shepherd; therefore, I shall not want for comfort.

"Thy rod and thy staff they comfort me" (v. 4).

WE ARE LIVING in a comfortless world. Everyone is so busy nursing his own hurts that he has very little time to bind up the hurts of others. This is a lonely loveless old world, and it's dying for a little bit of love.

Into this situation comes the Lord Jesus to offer Himself to the child of God as a Shepherd of comfort and sustaining grace in the hour of human sorrow.

I am confident that multitudes know just how deeply the plowshare of sorrow can drive into one's life. The thing I am concerned about is whether they have come to know what Jesus Christ can do in the hour when the sun blinks out and all the stars fade from their sky of hope. I am anxious that they shall know the gracious, sustaining ministry of the Shepherd when sorrow, adversity, bereavement and disappointment are breaking the speed limit in their lives.

It is in the hour of our deepest sorrow that we most frequently discover just how gracious and sustaining our Shepherd really is! There are some things about the Lord Jesus Christ which can never be discovered in the light. Some of the sweetest and most precious realities of the Saviour are to be found *only in the shadows*. When in my busy life as a pastor I was called into a home where sorrow had entered, I invariably prayed, "Precious Saviour, help these dear ones to find out something about Thyself which they never could have known apart from this experience."

In Isaiah 43:1-3 the Lord in speaking to His own says: "I have called thee by thy name; thou art mine. When thou passest through the waters, I will be with thee; and through the rivers, they shall not overflow thee: when thou walkest through the fire, thou shalt not be burned; neither shall the flame kindle upon thee. For I am the LORD thy God, the Holy One of Israel, thy Saviour: I gave Egypt for thy ransom, Ethiopia and Seba for thee."

These verses do not promise immunity from sorrow. They do not guarantee that the floods and fires of sorrow and affliction will not come; but they do guarantee that when they come, the Shepherd will go through them with us and will see to it that the floods do not overflow and that the flames do not kindle upon us. He proved that He was as good as His word in Noah's day and in the day of the three Hebrew children. He is still proving every hour of every day that He is as good as His word.

This intimate association of Himself with us in

our sorrow is beautifully set before us in Psalm 147:3-4, "He healeth the broken in heart and bindeth up their wounds. He telleth the number of the stars; he calleth them all by their names." Two more widely separated spheres could hardly be imagined—*shining heavenly stars and broken human hearts!* In the one, we are taken on an excursion through the starry heavens. We are called upon to take note of the uncountable millions of celestial bodies reaching out into uncountable billions of miles in space, and there we are introduced to a Being who knows their exact number and the name of every one of them. We quail before such a Being. We fall upon our faces in fear and terror as we glimpse the majestic presence of the *God of Stars.*

The contrasting sphere is that of broken human hearts. It is as though the floor of heaven had suddenly opened and dropped us down to earth, but not into the homes and halls of earth where mirth and happiness reign. We crash on down through all of that into the very depths of human experience where broken hearts and blasted lives lie all around us. And here in this realm, too, strangely enough, we find God at work. Not now making and naming a few new stars, the greatness of which *drives us from Him* in awful *fear,* but healing and comforting broken hearts and binding up their wounds with a tenderness that *draws us to Him* and causes us to pillow our head upon His breast while with His own nail-pierced hand of love, He wipes every tear from our eyes.

For years I struggled with these two verses trying

to understand why two realms so vastly different
and so infinitely far apart were crowded into one
breath in the inspired Scriptures. Then one day I
learned the truth. It was in 1920 when, in eleven
short months, four of my most precious ones on
earth were, one after the other, suddenly snatched
from me in death. It was in those hours of darkness
that could be felt, shut away alone in my study by
day and my room by night, that I learned what God
the Lord was trying to say to me by putting these
two verses so close together and yet dealing with
realms so far apart. I learned in that black night
that God was trying to teach me that the *God of
stars IS the God of broken hearts.*

In our experiences of sorrow we are apt to feel
that God is so far away, that He is so busy number-
ing and naming stars and manipulating His vast
universe that He has no time to hear our feeble
gasp, as with uncontrollable sorrow we turn our
tear-stained faces to the sky, begging for some relief for our aching hearts. What God would have us
to know from these verses is that He is never so
busy manipulating the universe, as vast and intri-
cate as it is, that He does not have time to come
into our little home and stand with us at the bed-
side of a loved one fast slipping away, and to travel
with us to sustain us at the open gravesides; then He
returns with us to our homes and walks with us in
all our ways, drying our tears, healing our hurts,
and sanctifying to us our sorrows.

It was such a God who left His stars to come
to the side of a brokenhearted Hagar when she

cried over the imminent death of her only son. It
was such a God who came to the desolate little
home in Moab where sat a brokenhearted Naomi,
thinking of the three graves which contained the
bodies of husband and two sons, and whispered in
her ear words of hope and blessing and restoration
back in the homeland of Bethlehem-Judah. It was
such a God who could leave His complex universe
and stand at the sealed tomb of Lazarus and weep,
and in the next moment open the tomb and bring
forth Lazarus. It is this God in the person of Christ
who is waiting today to walk straight into the very
heart of your sorrow and heal it by the touch of
His nail-pierced hand. The Lord is my Shepherd,
therefore I shall not want for *comfort*.

Verse 4 of this Twenty-third Psalm has a wonderful outline of what the Christian view of death is:

I. It is a *possibility*, not a *certainty*—"Yea,
though I walk . . . ."

II. It is a *calm walk*, not a *frantic race*.

III. It is a *shadow*, not a *reality*. The truth of
this was beautifully brought out by a nine-year-old
boy when I was examining him for baptism. I said,
"Donn, what is the relationship of baptism to the
death, burial and resurrection of Christ?" He
answered, "In baptism we go through all the mo-
tions Jesus went through but we don't have any of
the feelings." Yes, thank God, He took all the *feelings* and left us with the *shadow*.

IV. It is a *secure* walk, not a *fearful* one.

V. It is a *companionship*, not a *lonely journey*.

VI. It is a *comfort*, not a *confusion*.

VII. It is a *transition*, not a *terminus*.

VIII. It is an *arrival home*, not a *stop on the way*. In Psalm 48:14 we are told that God will be our *Guide even unto death* and also that He will be our *God forever*.

9

Supply

The Lord is my Shepherd; therefore, I shall not want for supply.

"Thou preparest a table before me" (v. 5).

IT IS THE RESPONSIBILITY of the Oriental shepherd to see that the sheep are led into places where there is plenty of food and water. The shepherd who frequently leads his sheep into places where he can "prepare no table before them" will soon be without a flock or a job. The sheep are incapable of finding pasture for themselves. The pasture must be prepared by the shepherd. How like us in this barren world!

And yet again, into this situation comes the Lord Jesus and offers Himself to the believer as a Shepherd who knows where the supply is and how to prepare it. Our Shepherd bears across His breast these wonderful words of assurance; "My God shall supply all your need according to his riches in glory by Christ Jesus." Truly the name of our God is El Shaddai, which means "the breasted one." He is the one from whom we draw our nourishment. He is the one who Himself is the source of all our supply.

We will go a long way when we come to understand that it is not so much a lot of "things" which the dear Saviour provides for us, as it is Himself. He is the great I Am. It is His blank check handed to every believing child of God, and all we need to do is fill it in. Do we need peace? Then He says, "I am thy peace." Do we need salvation? He says, "I am thy salvation." Do we need comfort? He says, "I am thy comfort." Do we need joy? He says, "I am thy joy." No, it is not a lot of "things" which the Lord gives us out of His infinite storehouse, but it is Himself.

This precious truth that it is the Lord Himself who becomes our supply is beautifully brought out in Isaiah 33. In this chapter the prophet has been describing the forlorn and forsaken condition of Israel because of her sin, and he declares that "the earth mourneth and languisheth: Lebanon is ashamed and hewn down: Sharon is like a wilderness; and Bashan and Carmel shake off their fruits." He then goes on to say that God is going to arise and exalt Himself, and that when He does, a fire shall devour them. In the midst of this prophecy of coming judgment, the prophet asks the question in verse 14, "Who among us shall dwell with the devouring fire? Who among us shall dwell with everlasting burnings?" Then in verse 15 he answers, "He that walketh righteously, and speaketh uprightly; he that despiseth the gain of oppressions, that shaketh his hands from holding of bribes, that stoppeth his ears from hearing of blood, and shutteth his eyes from seeing evil." In verse 16 the prophet continues in the following words, "He shall dwell on high: his place of defence shall be the munitions of rocks; bread shall be given him; his waters shall be sure."

Here we are told that the man of righteousness who is here described is to "dwell on high" and that "his place of defense shall be the munitions of rocks" and that "his bread shall be given him and his waters shall be sure."

It is interesting here to study the full significance of this term "munitions of rocks." A careful study of the Hebrew word here translated *rocks* will indicate that this is not a pile of rather small rocks that the beleaguered soldier may pick up and throw at his enemy, but rather it is a cleft in the side of one great towering rock. In fact, the better translation is "craggy heights."

This truth of our munitions of rocks being a craggy height is beautifully brought out in Exodus 17 and Numbers 20. In Exodus 17, when Israel thirsted, God told Moses to *strike* the rock. He did so and water came forth. Later, when Israel thirsted again, as recorded in Numbers 20, God told Moses to *speak* to the rock. Moses, unfortunately, displayed a little temper and smote it instead, for which he was disciplined because all he needed to do was to speak to it and the water would have flowed. It is interesting and instructive to know that the Hebrew word translated *rock* in Exodus 17 is a word which means an imbedded rock, rather a flat rock, submerged rock, having in it the picture of humiliation and abasement. What a blessed picture of Christ, the Rock who was smitten for us. We read of Him in Philippians 2, "Who, being in the form of God, thought it not robbery to be equal with God: but made himself of no reputation, and took upon him the form of a servant, and was made in the likeness of men: and being found in fashion as a man, he humbled himself, and became obedient unto death, even the death of the cross." It was this humbled Man, this Man who had been brought down, this Man who was "imbedded" in humanity that was smitten upon Calvary's cross, and in the smiting provided the river of salvation which flows for every believing heart.

It is further interesting and instructive to discover that in Numbers 20 there is a different Hebrew word used and translated *rock*. It is a Hebrew word which means lofty, craggy heights. This is in contradistinction to the low, imbedded, flat rock. It is this lofty, craggy height, this exalted, towering mountainpeak of granite that is to be *spoken to* and the waters will flow. What a beautiful picture of our Lord we have in the change of the Hebrew word here, and how it reminds us of Philippians 2 again as we continue the description of our Lord in verse 9: "Wherefore God also hath highly exalted him, and given him a name which is above every name: that at the name of Jesus every knee should bow, of things in heaven, and things in earth, and things under the earth; and that every tongue should confess that Jesus Christ is Lord, to the glory of God the Father"! Paul tells us that this Rock back yonder in the wilderness, in both cases, was Christ (1 Co 10:4).

Now we begin to see what Isaiah, through the inspiration of the Spirit, had in mind when he said that God's man, God's child, dwells in the munitions of craggy heights. There we are, beloved, not skulking behind a pile of small rocks which we must manipulate, but instead, hiding in the Rock of Ages cleft for us—there in the towering, rocky, granite heights of the risen, exalted and glorified Saviour resides every child of God.

We have pointed out this peculiar and blessed description of the "munitions of rocks" in order that we might now point up the application of it all to our theme, namely, "The Lord is my Shepherd; therefore, I shall not want for *supply*." The reader will be reminded that the one who is dwelling in this cleft in the craggy heights is to have his bread given him, and his water will be sure. Is someone saying today, "Well, when one is isolated away yonder in the craggy heights, could he not be made subject to such a prolonged siege that he would die of starvation? How is he to get out for bread and water?" Ah, blessed truth! The promise is that his bread shall be given him and his water shall be sure.

But from whence will the water and the bread come? We would remind you that the Lord Jesus Christ said, "I am the bread of life," and He is also the water of life. Yes, by some glorious, mystical operation of the sovereign grace of God, He who surrounds us with Himself as the Rock and protects

us from every harm and danger and enemy—it is
He Himself who becomes our water and our bread.
Reach out, beleagured child of God, and take the
Rock and you will discover that it becomes bread.
Reach out and take the Rock, and you will discover
that it becomes water. *Thou preparest a table be-
fore me.* History tells us much of the *cliff* dwellers.
Why not let us Christians make a new historical
record and become *cleft* dwellers.

How often the child of God is caused to doubt
whether or not the Shepherd either can, or will,
prepare a table of adequate supply in the hour of
deepest human need! Such an experience is revealed
in chapter 6 of John's gospel. The Lord Jesus had
led His disciples apart for a little rest. According
to Mark's statement concerning this event, the Lord
is reported as saying, "Come ye yourselves apart
. . . and rest a while." Or, as Vance Havner puts it,
you *will* come apart. But no sooner were they in
the place apart, that the multitudes were there. The
gospel records indicate that the Lord Jesus taught
them all day long, and at eventide, as Jesus looked
over the vast multitude, He knew that they must
have something to eat. According to John 6:5, He
said to Phillip, "Whence shall we buy bread, that
these may eat?" Verse 6 is enlightening here, for
it reads, "And this he said to prove him [Philip]:
for he himself knew what he would do."

Yes, the Shepherd knew what He was going to
do, but He was seeking to elicit from the disciple an
expression of faith that would indicate that Philip
knew that however impossible the situation seemed

to be, the Lord Jesus Christ would have the answer.
But the expression of faith for which the Lord
Jesus Christ was seeking was not forthcoming. Instead, Philip said "Two hundred pennyworth of
bread is not sufficient for them, that every one of
them may take a little."

You can almost hear the tone of helpless and
hopeless unbelief which nearly amounts to a criticism of the Lord for even thinking that they could
possibly supply the need of so many. The contagion
of unbelief is evidenced here in the next two verses,
where we read that Andrew caught the idea, and
said, "There is a lad here, which hath five barley
loaves, and two small fishes: but what are they
among so many?" One can almost hear the same
undertone of criticism in the statement of Andrew.

Here were two of His beloved disciples from
whom Jesus was seeking to elicit an expression of
faith which would declare that no matter how impossible the situation, no matter how large the
crowd, and no matter how small the supply, their
Shepherd was the God of the impossible. But the
desired response of faith was not forthcoming, so
the Lord turned at once to the business at hand and
did what He had intended to do all the time—He
prepared a table before them.

When faced with the impossible, Philip and Andrew failed; but let us not criticize them overmuch.
Rather, let each one of us look into the mirror and
say, "Thou art the man." Have there not been a
thousand times and more in the lives of all of us
when we have been confronted suddenly with an

impossible situation, and faith refused to rise in the hour of need and lay hold upon the Shepherd as the one who could supply the need? The doorbell rings, or a special-delivery letter is handed to us, or a Western Union telegram arrives, confronting us suddenly with a situation which is infinitely beyond us. What do we do in an hour like this? Do we throw up our hands in utter helplessness and say that we have nothing with which to meet the need of the hour, and look in helpless despondency all around us, succumbing to a terrible defeat? Or, do we take the thing as from Him and believe that He has sent this to us with the express purpose of testing us to see what we would do? Oh, for the experience in our hearts of calmly sitting down in the green pastures and watching Him do the impossible as He prepares a table before us in the supply of every need!

It is sweetly significant here that in the gospel records we are told that there was not only *grass* for them to sit upon, but that it was *green* grass. Surely the Spirit of God who inspired this record must have wanted to call our attention to this wonderful Twenty-third Psalm in which we are told that we are to lie down in *green* pastures. Surely there must have been some connection in the divine mind in informing us that the grass here was green. The purpose is so very evident. The green pastures of Psalm 23, where He prepares His table for us, so often are the places of our utter impossibility. So often the same frustrating situation which confronted Philip and Andrew that day confronts us, and the dear Lord wants us to know that the green pastures of Psalm 23 and the tables that He prepares in them are the tables of supply when our extremity of need has been reached. There is no way up, there's no way out, there's no way around; unless God does something for us, it will be the end. Then it is that He prepares the table before us.

Surely the Shepherd's table is bountifully laden. Some years ago I began compiling a list of things that we have in the Lord Jesus Christ—things that the Lord Jesus Christ Himself becomes to the believing heart. We are indebted to many sources for the final compilation, but may we contemplate what we have in the Lord Jesus Christ:

In Jesus Christ we have a life that can never be forfeited.

In Jesus Christ we have a relation that can never be abrogated.

In Jesus Christ we have a righteousness that can never be tarnished.

In Jesus Christ we have an acceptance that can never be questioned.

In Jesus Christ we have a judgment that can never be repeated.

In Jesus Christ we have a title that can never be clouded.

In Jesus Christ we have a position that can never be invalidated.

In Jesus Christ we have a standing that can never be disputed.

In Jesus Christ we have a justification that can never be reversed.

In Jesus Christ we have a seal that can never be violated.

In Jesus Christ we have an inheritance that can never be alienated.

In Jesus Christ we have a wealth that can never be depleted.

In Jesus Christ we have a resource that can never be diminished.

In Jesus Christ we have a bank that can never be closed.

In Jesus Christ we have a possession that can never be measured.

In Jesus Christ we have a portion that can never be denied.

In Jesus Christ we have a peace that can never be destroyed.

In Jesus Christ we have a joy that can never be suppressed.

In Jesus Christ we have a love that can never be abated.

In Jesus Christ we have a grace that can never be arrested.

In Jesus Christ we have a strength that can never be vitiated.

In Jesus Christ we have a power that can never be exhausted.

In Jesus Christ we have a salvation that can never be annulled.

In Jesus Christ we have a forgiveness that can never be rescinded.

In Jesus Christ we have a deliverance that can never be thwarted.

In Jesus Christ we have an assurance that can never be disappointed.

In Jesus Christ we have a nature that can never be changed.

In Jesus Christ we have an access that can never be discontinued.

In Jesus Christ we have an attraction that can never be superseded.

In Jesus Christ we have a comfort that can never be lessened.

In Jesus Christ we have a service that can never be unrewarded.

In Jesus Christ we have an Intercessor who can never be disqualified.

In Jesus Christ we have a revelation that can never be destroyed.

In Jesus Christ we have a Victor who can never be vanquished.

In Jesus Christ we have a resurrection that can never be hindered.

In Jesus Christ we have a hope that can never be disappointed.

In Jesus Christ we have a glory that can never be dimmed.

Yes, Christ is all. Christ is all in the Father's vision. Christ is all in the Spirit's message. Christ is all in the Scripture's pages. Christ is all in creation's morning. Christ is all in sin's midnight. Christ is all in atoning grace. Christ is all and in all.

This is the table which He prepares for us in the green pastures of otherwise insurmountable and unsolvable difficulties. Surely we can say with David, "The Lord is my Shepherd, therefore I shall not want for *supply*."

10

Protection

The Lord is my Shepherd; therefore I shall not want for protection.
"In the presence of mine enemies" (v. 5).

IN CHAPTER 9 we looked at the *supply* which the Lord Jesus as our Shepherd provides for every one of His sheep. We saw how He "prepares a table before us." As glorious as all of this was and is, it would mean very little to the hungry sheep if there were no protection afforded him while he ate. Not too much use in "preparing a table" for the sheep when a multitude of enemies are surrounding that table determined to keep the sheep from ever reaching it. But the blessed revelation of our psalm is that this table is prepared for us in the very presence of our enemies, and that carries with it the assurance that He who prepares the table will protect His sheep while they eat.

In the Oriental shepherd life, it would be next to impossible for a shepherd always to prepare his table for his flock in some sequestered nook where no wild animals or venomous serpents could make their appearance. Therefore it is necessary for the shepherd to prepare the table for his flock in the very presence of these enemies, in which case the shepherd himself must be the refuge and protection of the sheep.

Sweetly and beautifully our Lord Jesus Christ fills this picture. He offers Himself to every believer as a Shepherd who is also the believer's refuge and protection. "Rock of Ages, cleft for me; let me hide myself in Thee." How wonderful to know that in the midst of a world in which we are literally surrounded by the wolves, bears, lions and serpents of the evil one, our precious Shepherd meets our every need, prepares our table with abundance, and stands omnipotent guard over every feeding sheep!

One of the terrible enemies which surrounds the table of every feeding sheep is sin itself. The awful and constant temptation which sin throws around the believing child of God is one of the most potent enemies known to the sheep of His pasture. But here in the midst of ten thousand temptations, the Lord Jesus Christ is the answer to this problem as well as to all others. Let us discuss temptation and how to meet it in the risen Christ who is our Shepherd.

We see all around us the terrible evidence of this fearful and awful thing, namely, the temptation of the human heart to sin. *Sin is an awful thing. One sin wrecked the universe.* And the nature of that one sin was not the degraded and debauched kind, but it was the sin which is still the most popular and little-thought-of sin in human experience. It was simply the sin of putting man's will in opposition to God's will. Adam and Eve were not tempted to drunkenness and debauchery. They were tempted to say yes when God said no. They yielded, and a wrecked universe is the result.

Back of every falsehood, back of every broken life, back of every disappointed heart, back of every blackened character, back of every broken home, back of every divorce court, back of every jail, back of every penitentiary, back of every electric chair and hangman's noose, back of every diseased body, back of every hospital sickbed, back of every open grave, back of every broken treaty, back of every bloody battlefield, back of the roar of cannon and whine of plane stands one awful thing —*sin*. But sin yielded to! It may be that you did not yield to it personally, but somebody did and you suffer the overall effect of another's sin. All of this broken and bleeding wreckage of humanity which we see strewn around us is the evidence of temptation which was not overcome.

But, in the midst of all this evidence of human defeat in the hour of sin's temptation, another record is being written of glorious victory—victory for every child of God who trusts the finished work of the crucified and risen Saviour. One of the most glorious declarations of inspired Scripture is that of Roman 6:14, "For sin shall not have dominion over you."

Talk about the "liberated countries" that have been taken from under the iron heel of the oppressor! Talk about the joy which fills the hearts of the liberated people! Talk about the terrible cost to bring about this deliverance! Well, *here* is a deliverance for you—not just a few nations here and there which were caught in the toils of the despoiler, but the whole world!

The inspired Scriptures declare in Romans 3:19, 23 that the whole world, including every individual in it, is guilty of sin. From the highest pinnacle of moral attainment to the lowest depths of immorality and drunkenness, every man and woman walks from day to day, shackled and fettered by the chains of sin. The only exceptions to this universal enslavement are the men and women who, through the grace of God, have had their sins forgiven and cleansed at crimson Calvary and are now made to be partakers of the risen life of the eternal Christ. To such, Scripture addresses itself: "Sin shall not have dominion over you." Here is a deliverance that is not confined to a few nations. Here is a deliverance that can be the blessed experience of every individual who will accept it. And a deliverance, too, which was brought about at a cost greater than all earthly battles combined. You *can* have victory over sin in the hour of its temptation if you want it.

The question which no doubt is arising in your mind is, "*How* can I have this victory?" Let us go straight to the heart of the matter and call your attention to a little and obscure word which is so seldom considered. It is that little word "reckon" in Romans 6:11. The whole verse reads as follows: "Likewise reckon ye also yourselves to be dead indeed unto sin, but alive unto God through Jesus

Christ our Lord." Here is a twofold statement. The truth here presented is that *both the death and the resurrection* of the Lord Jesus Christ are potentially and positionally ours the moment we believe on Christ. In other words, God reckons that when Christ died, I died. He likewise reckons that when Christ arose, I arose.

Romans 6:6 goes straight to the heart of the matter when it declares, "Knowing this, that our old man is crucified with him"—the old man in this case being another name for our old sinful nature. Now if God in heaven reckons that it was I who died in the person of my Substitute back on Calvary's cross, then I should "likewise reckon." The result of such reckoning would be that I would not be yielding to sin when it comes upon me with its fiery temptations. If I reckon myself to be *dead*, how then can I sin? *It is just in proportion to my failure to thus reckon that sin has sway in my Christian life.*

The principle I am trying to make clear is set forth in the following illustration. Two young ladies were saved one night in a revival meeting. Two or three days later they received an invitation to a dance. Feeling instinctively that the dance, as they knew it, did not fit into things as they now knew them, they sought the Lord's guidance in the matter. In leafing through the Scriptures for some help, they came upon Colossians 3:3, "For ye are dead, and your life is hid with Christ in God."

"That's the answer," they said and, turning the

invitation over, wrote across the back of it, "Sorry we cannot come, we are dead."

Yes, it is just as simple as that. God reckons you to be dead to sin. *When you reckon likewise, then victory is yours.*

But this is only half of the picture in Romans 6:11. We are not only dead to sin through the Lord Jesus Christ, *but we are alive to righteousness* through the Lord Jesus Christ. Therefore, just as I *will not be yielding* to the temptation to sin if I reckon myself to be dead to sin, so conversely, I *will be yielding* myself to righteousness if I reckon myself to be alive in Christ. Since I cannot do the things I am dead to, it necessarily follows that I can do the things which I am alive to. God reckons me to be dead to sin and alive to righteousness. When I agree with God and reckon as He reckons, the battle is over, the victory is won, and sin's power is broken.

Thus the Lord Jesus not only prepares the table but is also our protection while we "eat" this blessed victory and sin looks on helplessly.

Not only is the feeding sheep surrounded by sin itself, but he is also surrounded by a thousand other enemies which can produce unrest, spiritual starvation, and eventual spiritual defeat unless he knows how to turn these "enemies" over to the Shepherd also. This protective ministry of our Shepherd is beautifully set forth in one of the Bible similes found in Isaiah 33:21, "But there the glorious LORD will be unto us a place of broad rivers and streams." In this beautiful simile of the Lord Jesus we hear

His assuring voice saying that in the midst of all these dangers He is still standing omnipotent guard.

In this simile in which God is likened to a river are found several helpful suggestions in connection with our present theme. In what way is God like a river? In the day in which Isaiah uttered these words, a river was the greatest and most effective source of protection known. A city or a province that had a river running by it or around it was almost impregnable. Years ago large estates had moats around them. A moat was just an overgrown ditch full of water, but it was a great protection to the estate around which it ran. And this is the very picture here in Isaiah.

This was at the time of the Assyrian invasion and Israel had been crowded within the beleagured walls of the city of Jerusalem. Sennacherib was waiting outside for them to give in to final surrender. It was then that Isaiah stood forth and declared that between those Assyrian soldiers and the walls of the beleagured city of Jerusalem there flowed the omnipotent God like a mighty invisible river. The Scriptures bear record of the fact that 180,000 of these Assyrian soldiers were "drowned" in this invisible river when one angel came down from heaven, and the next morning the Assyrians were "all dead corpses." When God said that He would be a place of broad rivers and streams to His people, He meant that He would be just that.

No doubt the military leaders of Israel in that day lamented the fact that Jerusalem was not located on a river. No doubt many of them felt that such a location would provide perfect protection. But Jerusalem wasn't located on a river, and it couldn't be moved. The only solution for Jerusalem was that a river could be brought to it. How often we, too, may feel that our difficulties and dangers could be removed if our environment could be changed, but it can't. It is in such hours and such experiences that God moves to us and flows around us like a river. Yea, like many rivers and streams combined. There in the midst of enemies, in the midst of temptations, in the midst of impossible situations, our Shepherd "prepares a table" and bids the trusting sheep to eat quietly and safely "in the presence of his enemies." The Lord is my Shepherd, therefore I shall not want for *protection*.

Let us look at one more assurance in the "green pastures" of the Scriptures. Psalm 27:1-3 says, "The Lord is my light and my salvation; whom shall I fear? The LORD is the strength of my life; of whom shall I be afraid? When the wicked, even mine enemies and my foes, came upon me to eat up my flesh, they stumbled and fell. Though an host should encamp against me, my heart shall not fear: though war should rise against me, in this will I be confident."

In verse 1 our Lord is presented in His threefold ministry. He is our "light," He is our "salvation," and He is our "strength."

Note that He is all of this in the same sequential order in which we came to know Him. First, He must be our "light." He finds us in the dark, but He does not leave us there. In 1 Peter 2:9 we are called "out of darkness into his marvellous light." In Ephesians 5:8 we find that we were not only *in* darkness, but that we *were* darkness: "For ye were sometimes darkness, but now are ye light."

Romans 1:21 says, "Their foolish heart was darkened." The cause of this darkness is *rejected light*. "When they knew God, they glorified him not as God." There is no darkness so great as rejected light. This fact is brought into focus in Matthew 6:23: "If therefore the light that is in thee be darkness, how great is that darkness!" This does not say that the light has gone out and darkness is the result. It says that the light *is in you* but it is great darkness. The only way light which is still shining can be darkness is for one to treat the light as though it wasn't there.

Let me illustrate. Suppose I go to a church to preach. I have never been in that building before. When I am through I go out to my car and I discover I left my Bible on the pulpit. I go back to the church and find that the caretaker has turned out all the lights. Now, how would I proceed to find my Bible in that strange building?

I check to see if one of the doors might still be unlocked. It is. I step inside and try to remember something about the arrangement of the auditorium. I remember that there were swinging doors out of the foyer into the center aisle of the auditorium. I feel my way along the wall until I find them. I move inside. I step very carefully until I find the back seat, then I go down the aisle, feeling the back of every seat. Finally I run out of seats. I remember there was a table, some chairs and a piano there, so I move cautiously until I find the platform. I remember that there was a short flight of steps at the edge of the platform. I slide my feet carefully across the floor until I find the steps. Then I have a difficult task ahead of me. I must not fall off the platform. I tiptoe and find the pulpit chairs and know that if I turn slightly to the left and take two or three steps I will just about come to the pulpit stand. I move, still carefully, and there it is—and there is my Bible lying upon it. Now I must retrace my steps in the same cautious manner.

That is the way I would have to move if the lights were all out and it was pitch-dark in that room. But, suppose when I came back to the church I met the caretaker who had turned out the lights coming out the door. He asks me what I want, and I tell him. He steps back inside and turns on the master switch and the entire building is as light as day.

How foolish would you think I was if, in the full blaze of that light, I proceeded exactly as I did when I came in the building when it was pitch-dark. You see, I am in the light, but I have rejected it and treated it as though it did not exist.

So it is with us. When Christ sheds His light upon our sinful ways and we reject it, then we are not only *in* darkness, but we *are* darkness. John 1:9 tells us He is "the true Light, which lighteth every man that cometh into the world."

The second thing the Psalm 27 text tells about Christ is that He is our salvation. Please note that it does not say He *gives* me salvation. It says He *is* my salvation. Salvation is not something which He hands to us and says, "Here is your salvation." If this is what He does it is no wonder that we lose our salvation every little while and then have to get saved all over again!

Salvation is not a "thing." It is a Person! It is the personal incoming of Christ into our hearts. *And you cannot lose Him!* When He is your salvation you are saved forever. We are made "one" with Him. We are "accepted" in Him (Eph 1:6). In 2 Peter 1:4 we are told that when we are saved we have received the very *nature* of God.

Our text in Psalm 27 says that in the third place Christ is the strength of our lives. The psalmist says that in view of all these three wonderful blessings, we need not fear our enemies. Twice in verse 3 He declares that there is none of whom we should be afraid. We are studying about "tables in the *presence* of our enemies." David not only told us in Psalm 23 that the Shepherd would prepare us such tables, but here in Psalm 27 he actually sits at the tables and laughs at his enemies.

Stop right now. Take your Bible and look at verse 2 of Psalm 27. Underscore the little word "they." It is very important to you. David says that when his enemies came upon him, "they stumbled and fell." When his enemies came upon him they expected to see him lying slaughtered and dead. When it was all over, *they* were the ones who were fallen and dead!

Now look at verse 3 of Psalm 27. Underscore the

words "in this will I be confident." David is saying that even if an "host" or "wars" should rise up against him, in *this* will he be confident. What is it that he is so confident about? The fact that they will "stumble" and "fall" and that he will be the only one standing up in victory.

Blessed be the tables which our Lord prepares. They are not back in the forests of a sequestered life, but out in the midst of a godless world where everyone can see what He puts on our tables. And seeing, they may have an appetite!

11

Power

The Lord is my shepherd; therefore I shall not want for power.

"Thou anointest my head with oil" (v. 5).

OIL IN THE SCRIPTURES is usually a symbol of the Holy Spirit. It was used in such a fashion when the high priest was anointed and inaugurated into office. It is the picture of the anointing of the Spirit of God for power in service.

Our Lord Jesus Christ comes to every child of God and offers Himself as the Shepherd of power. How weak we are! How futile our puny efforts! But how different it is when the power of God is operating through us!

There stands a fifty-car freight train with a mammoth engine attached. The conductor gives the signal, the engineer opens the throttle—and nothing happens. The fireman had forgotten to get up steam. Eventually steam is generated and the cylinders are throbbing for release. The conductor gives the signal, the engineer opens the throttle, the mighty wheels begin to move, the drawheads tighten, and the engine moves down the track as though it were hauling toothpicks. Same engine, same everything, plus *power!*

There lies a one hundred-foot length of three-inch pipe. It is filled with water and plugged at both ends. Someone knocks the plug out of the lower end, and the water flows out of the pipe with not enough force to disturb the gravel at the mouth of the pipe. But put a hydraulic pump on one end of that pipe, remove the plug at the other end, give it the power of the hydraulic pump, and the water in that pipe will blast the windows out of the house across the street. Same pipe, same water, same everything—plus *power!*

A beautiful and modern trolley car stands on the tracks in the middle of a busy street. It is loaded with passengers. It is the latest model, but it is stalled. The trolley connection is off the wire, and nothing happens when the motorman opens the throttle. The conductor steps off the platform, pulls the trolley arm down, and then brings it up underneath the wire that carries the mighty power of electricity from a distant dynamo. The motors hum, the motorman opens the throttle, and the streetcar moves off down the track. Same trolley car, same motorman, same conductor, same everything plus *power!*

Many a Christian life is "dead" on the rails—impotent in its flow or stalled on the tracks. But let the anointing of the Shepherd touch that life, and things begin to happen. Same Christian, same everything, plus *power!*

A wonderful picture of the truth we are here dealing with is in 2 Kings 13:14-19:

> Now Elisha was fallen sick of his sickness whereof he died. And Joash the king of Israel came down unto him, and wept over his face, and said, O my father, my father, the chariot of Israel, and the horsemen thereof.
>
> And Elisha said unto him, Take bow and arrows. And he took unto him bow and arrows. And he said to the king of Israel, Put thine hand upon the bow. And he put his hand upon it; and Elisha put his hands upon the king's hands.
>
> And he said, Open the window eastward. And he opened it. Then Elisha said, Shoot. And he shot. And he said, The arrow of the LORD's deliverance, and the arrow of deliverance from Syria; for thou shalt smite the Syrians in Aphek, till thou have consumed them.
>
> And he said, Take the arrows. And he took them. And he said unto the king of Israel, Smite upon the ground. And he smote thrice, and stayed.
>
> And the man of God was wroth with him, and said, Thou shouldest have smitten five or six times; then hadst thou smitten Syria till thou hadst consumed it; whereas now thou shalt smite Syria but thrice.

In this thrilling Old Testament story is the picture of communicated power. The prophet's hands were laid upon the king's hand for only a moment. It was but a momentary touch, but it was the symbol of the communicated power which the king needed and which the prophet of God could give.

Here we have a perfect picture of the Christian and his communicated power promised in Acts 1:8: "Ye shall receive power, after that the Holy Ghost is come upon you"! What a picture it is of the truth of 1 Chronicles 29:12: "In thine hand is power and might and in thine hand it is to make great, and to give strength unto all"!

This story in 2 Kings also reveals the fact that this communicated power comes by personal contact. Elisha actually touched the hands of the king. Truly it is no idle talk when we profess that our spirits are in touch with His Spirit. Oh, for the touch of the hand of the Shepherd which has the ability to make great and to give strength unto all! Have we really *touched* the mighty Saviour, or have we just *thronged* Him?

In the gospel record (Mt 9:20-22) is the story of a woman who had been ill for a long time. Hearing that Jesus was passing by, she determined to get close enough to touch Him. She was sure that if she could accomplish this, she would be made whole. The story goes on to tell how this frail woman kept pressing through the throng until at last she was close enough to reach her hand through between two great burly figures of protecting disciples. Touching the hem of the Saviour's garment, she was immediately made whole.

The interesting part of the story, however, is found in what Jesus did and said. He stopped immediately. He turned around and said, "Who touched me?" At once His disciples called His attention to the fact that people had been thronging

Him all day long, that there were probably dozens, if not hundreds, of people who had touched Him in the milling multitudes that day. But had they *really touched* Him? Apparently they had just *thronged* Him.

But when this one woman really touched Him in faith, He knew something had happened because He perceived that virtue had gone out from Him. How is it with you? Have you been traveling with the Saviour these many years but are still weak and powerless?

You have thronged Him all day long, again and again and again. You have been found in His company, you have united with His church, you are engaged in His service, perhaps, and yet the same old weakness of sin's overpowering mastery dogs your steps every day like a tyrant.

Here is the secret. Perhaps you have just been thronging and have never really touched Him. It is the touch of His hand that can make great and give power that is needed in our lives. How about it? May we ask ourselves the question again, "Have we simply thronged Him, or have we really touched Him so that virtue has come forth from Him and into us?"

It is perfectly possible to know Him in contact for salvation and still know nothing of contact with Him through the Spirit for power in daily service. Why do we have powerless churches and powerless Christians in the face of the promise of Acts 1:8? What could God not do if His own powerless ones

What could God not do if His own powerless ones
would come into contact with Him for this promised
power?

Another lesson learned from this story on 2
Kings is that communicated power comes before
the act of service is required. The prophet first
touched the king's hands, and then he told him to
shoot. Our risen Lord never requires a service of us
but what He first equips us with power to perform
it. God never asks any man or any woman under
any circumstances to be or do anything for Him
without at that moment placing at his disposal am-
ple and adequate provision to be and to do that
thing. God's commandments are God's enablements.

The truth we are now dealing with is blessedly
pictured in several instances in the New Testament.
We would remind you of the story of the crippled
man at the pool of Bethesda (Jn 5:12-16). The
story is that at a certain hour the waters in the pool
of Bethesda were moved, and whoever went in first
was healed. The Lord Jesus passed by this powerless man, looked down in pity upon him, and said
"Wilt thou be made whole?"

The man replied, "Sir, I have no man, when the
water is troubled, to put me into the pool: but
while I am coming, another steppeth down before
me."

It was then that the Lord Jesus said to him,
"Rise, take up thy bed, and walk."

Remember what the man then said? Remember
how he looked up into the face of the Lord and
said, "Sir, that is exactly what I want to do. If I

could get up from this bed and take it home, I
would have done it long ago. I would not have
waited for You to come and tell me to do it. It
ought to be very obvious to You, sir, that You have
asked me to do an impossible thing. If I could, I
would; but I can't."

No, there is nothing like this in the record in the
gospels. The only place that you find that kind of
record is in your own life. When faced with some
certain command from the Lord Jesus, you have
answered by trying to argue with the Lord that you
are not equipped to do it, you are not able to do it,
you are not cut out to do it—you would love to do
it if you could, but you can't. No, such a baseless
argument or excuse is not to be found in Scripture.
That kind of business is found in the life of the
powerless Christian himself.

But what *do* we find in the Scripture record?
"And immediately he took up his bed, and walked."
Just like that. You see, with the command had come
the enabling. When the Lord Jesus dropped those
words onto the auditory nerves of the man's ears,
He also dropped power into the paralyzed body to
do what He told him to do. Five split seconds before, the man would have been perfectly on the
side of truth if he had said, "I want to, but I can't."
But when the Lord Jesus commanded him to, that
statement was no longer true, for God's commandment was God's enablement.

Let us take another New Testament illustration
of this principle. Walking in the temple one day,
the Lord Jesus saw a man with his hand and arm

all withered up at his side. He stepped in front of him and said, "Stretch forth thine hand."

Remember the strange answer that the man gave the Lord Jesus, when he said, "Sir, I'd love to do that, but I can't. I've been trying all my life long to make this withered hand go out there with the same punch and vigor that the other one does, but I just can't do it. I would if I could, but I can't."

No, you remember no such argument. That argument is not found in the pages of the divine record. It is found in the lives of powerless, disobedient, unwilling Christians. The record of the Scriptures is that the man stretched forth his hand. God's commandment was God's enablement.

Five seconds before, the man could have honestly said, "I can't." But when the Lord of power told him to do it, he could. And so with weak, defeated, baffled, powerless Christians. God speaks to you and orders you to do this or that, and you spend your time arguing back that you can't. You have failed to recognize the fact that what was true of you a few moments ago is no longer true, if in the meantime the Lord Jesus has requested or commanded that you do thus and so.

Another precious lesson confronting us in the story of 2 Kings is that communicated power is realized in the act of obedience. Naturally the presence of power is unrealized until used. The paralyzed man at the pool of Bethesda would have been lying there to the day of his death, and would never have known that he could get up and take his bed and walk. The only way he found it out was to make the effort of obedience. The moment he did, he discovered in amazement that the empowering had come with the ordering.

The man in the temple with the withered hand could have gone on to his grave, saying, "I can't, I can't" and would never have known that he could, had he not made the effort of obedience. Our churches are full to overflowing with born-again believers who are saying, "I can't, I can't." They do not know that what they think they cannot do, they could do if they would make the effort of obedience. They would be perhaps the most surprised people in the membership of their entire church to discover that the very thing they think impossible, they can do if they will obey.

What a tragedy! Multiplied thousands of Christians are going on to their graves, and going to meet Jesus Christ at the judgment seat of works not knowing that they are carrying with them all the time the power to be victors instead of victims. And the only reason they don't know it is because they refuse to make the effort of obedience. Yes, Christ gives what He commands. He empowers as we obey.

The Lord is my Shepherd, therefore I shall not want for *power*. "Thou anointest my head with oil."

12

Mercy

The Lord is my Shepherd, therefore, I shall not want for goodness *and* mercy.

"My cup runneth over. Surely goodness and mercy shall follow me all the days of my life" (vv. 5-6).

DON'T LOOK NOW, but you are being followed! By whom? By "goodness" and "mercy"! And if you will wait for them they will catch up with you.

We live on such a poverty-stricken plane while at the same time goodness and mercy are following us with outstretched hands to give us every blessing which God has stored up for us in the person of our blessed Shepherd, even the Lord Jesus Christ.

The blessed truth that the cup of the Christian may be constantly overflowing with the goodness and mercy of God is one of the outstanding revelations of Scripture. Perhaps this truth may be brought more clearly into focus if we look at it through the lens of some New Testament passages.

In Hebrews 9:15-17 we read: "And for this cause he is the mediator of the new testament, that by means of death, for the redemption of the transgressions that were under the first testament, they which

117

are called might receive the promise of eternal inheritance. For where a testament is, there must also of necessity be the death of the testator. For a testament is of force after men are dead: otherwise it is of no strength at all while the testator liveth."

Here we are told that the Lord Jesus Christ executed His last will and testament. Four or five observations concerning wills may serve to help us as we seek to find the Spirit's lessons for us in connection with the last will and testament of our Lord.

First, a will must name the heirs to the inheritance. Are you interested in knowing whether or not you are an heir in the last will and testament of Jesus Christ? Suppose today's paper had announced the death of John D. Rockefeller, Jr., and that he had left his entire estate of $500 million to one hundred residents of Cook County, Illinois. This would mean that one hundred people in Cook County, which includes the city of Chicago, would be the recipients of $5 million each. The will, however, provides that it is to be read from the steps of the city hall in New York City tomorrow at 6 P.M., and at that time the names of the heirs will be made public. The will further provides that unless the persons named are there at the time of the reading, they will forfeit their share of the inheritance.

Can one imagine a single human being left in the entire Cook County? The millions of residents of this county would be filling the highways and every conceivable means of transportation in their mad scramble to be in New York at six o'clock tomorrow, for who knows—any one of them might be among the one hundred. Surely in such a case there would be no lack of interest to determine whether or not one was an heir.

Well, John D. Rockefeller, Jr., did not die. *But Jesus Christ did!* And He named the heirs to His estate. Now if you are interested in knowing whether or not your name appears among the heirs, turn to Romans 8:15-17. There it is declared, "For ye have not received the spirit of bondage again to fear; but ye have received the Spirit of adoption, whereby we cry, Abba, Father. The Spirit itself beareth witness with our spirit, that we are the children of God: and if children, then heirs; heirs of God, and joint-heirs with Christ; if so be that we suffer with him, that we may be also glorified together." Are you named? Are you a child of God? Have you been born of His Spirit? If so, you are one of the heirs!

The *second* thing which a will must do is to describe the inheritance. The inheritance which is the portion of every believer is described on almost every page of the blessed Book; but like all other great truths, it will be found concentrated and brought down to pinpoint focus in one place. Look now at Ephesians 1:1-14:

> Paul, an apostle of Jesus Christ by the will of God, to the saints which are at Ephesus, and to the faithful in Christ Jesus: Grace be to you, and peace, from God our Father, and from the Lord Jesus Christ. Blessed be the God and Father of our Lord Jesus Christ, who hath blessed us with

all spiritual blessings in heavenly places in Christ: According as he hath chosen us in him before the foundation of the world, that we should be holy and without blame before him in love: having predestinated us unto the adoption of children by Jesus Christ to himself, according to the good pleasure of his will, to the praise of the glory of his grace, wherein he hath made us accepted in the beloved. In whom we have redemption through his blood, the forgiveness of sins, according to the riches of his grace; wherein he hath abounded toward us in all wisdom and prudence; having made known unto us the mystery of his will, according to his good pleasure which he hath purposed in himself: that in the dispensation of the fulness of times he might gather together in one all things in Christ, both which are in heaven, and which are on earth; even in him: . . . That we should be to the praise of his glory, who first trusted in Christ. In whom ye also trusted, after ye heard the word of truth, the gospel of your salvation: in whom also after that ye believed, ye were sealed with that holy Spirit of promise, which is the earnest of our inheritance until the redemption of the purchased possession, unto the praise of his glory.

Here it seems the provisions of Christ's last will and testament are listed in detail. The believer is (1) blessed with all spiritual blessings in heavenly places in Christ (v. 3), (2) chosen in Him before the foundation of the world (v. 4), (3) predestinated (v. 5), (4) adopted (v. 5), (5) accepted in the beloved (v. 6), (6) redeemed (v. 7), (7) forgiven (v. 7), (8) enlightened (v. 9), (9) enriched (v. 11), (10) sealed (vv. 13-14).

Surely this is the overflowing cup held in the outstretched hands of goodness and mercy. Look at the first item. If there were no other provisions in the last will and testament of the Lord Jesus Christ, this one alone would be sufficient—"Blessed with all spiritual blessings."

Let us not drain off the force of this wonderful statement by confining these blessings to only those things in our lives which we call "spiritual needs." We believe that this expression "all spiritual blessings" refers to every blessing ever needed in the entire life of a believer.

We do not agree with the popular contention that there is a "material" and a "spiritual" side in a believer's life. It is our opinion that the doctor's bill, the dentist's bill, the grocer's bill, and all other bills incident to the life of a believer are included in "spiritual blessings" just as much as the imponderables and the invisibles. The moment one becomes a born-again child of God he is a "spiritual" entity. He is born from heaven, his citizenship is in heaven, his conversation is in heaven, his family register is in heaven, his abode is in heaven, his destination is heaven, and he is a member of a body whose Head is already in heaven. *He is a heavenly individual.* And, as such, he is spiritual.

There are no two "closets" in his life—one marked "material" and one marked "spiritual"—in which he keeps his need for joy, peace, comfort, etc. His so-called material needs are just as much a concern to his heavenly Father as are his spiritual needs, and every need has been foreseen. *Surely my cup runneth over, and goodness and mercy shall follow me all the days of my life.*

Remember, it is "all" the days. It is the truth of Romans 8:28: "All things work *together* for good to them that love God." Don't forget the word *together!* Many things and many days taken by themselves and pulled out of the context of life may look as though they were characterized by anything but goodness and mercy. But when you put *all* the days and *all* the things *together* and they are seen in their relationship one to the other, and the overall perspective is taken into consideration, the child of God will be compelled to confess that it was goodness and mercy *all* the days.

The *third* provision, common to all wills, is that they must be probated. That is, a court must rule upon the validity of the will. Psalm 119:89 reads: "For ever, O Lord, thy word is settled in heaven." So the will which we are here discussing has been approved by the highest court in the universe.

The *fourth* thing about a will is that it is of no force until the one who makes it dies. The heirs could be absolutely penniless unless and until the one who makes the will dies. In the will now under discussion, that provision has been met also, for Christ did die and thereby released the provisions of His will.

The *fifth* provision of a will is that it must provide for an executor. Someone must be named to see to it that every heir named in the will gets exactly what the will left to him. The will under discussion here meets this requirement in a very strange and startling fashion. The record is that the Lord Jesus Christ made a will. He named the heirs. He described the inheritance. The will has been approved, and then He died to release its provisions.

But instead of turning the execution of His will over to someone else, He Himself rose from the dead to be the executor of His own will! He lives today to see to it that every believer gets exactly what is coming to him in His will, and the only person who can keep the believer from enjoying his inheritance is the believer himself. May it be said of every reader, "My cup runneth over. Surely *goodness* and *mercy* shall follow me all the days of my life."

13

Forever

The Lord is my Shepherd; therefore, I shall not want forever.

"I will dwell in the house of the LORD for ever" (v. 6).

IN CHAPTER 12 we pointed out the fact that we would not want for any good thing here and now, that goodness and mercy were following us all the days of our lives. Now, for a little while, let us consider together the comforting thought that eternity itself will never hold for us a single moment of need of any kind, except that which is *already supplied* by the Saviour-Shepherd.

Eternity is an awfully long time! The human mind is utterly incapable of even starting to comprehend its immensity. We are so accustomed to looking for the end of everything.

No sooner is the baby born than it begins its march toward the end of its life. No sooner do we hang up the calendar for the new year than we begin to look for the end of the first week. And then before we know it, it is time to tear off the first page. The first month has ended. And almost before we are aware of it we are down to December—the end of another year.

Everything with which we have to do is measured by time. It is extremely difficult for us to think in terms of eternity. It is, however, a comforting thought to know that our Shepherd is the God who inhabiteth eternity. That is, this thing that we call "time" down here is just part of eternity with Him. It is a blessed and comforting thought to know that our God of eternity has lived this very day in which we are now living in time. He has already lived it before us, and we are just catching up to Him.

Yes, our Shepherd has been along the way before us. He has lived this very day which surrounds us with its heartaches, its problems, its disappointments, its failures, as well as its joys and victories. He has been here. He knows all about it. This "day" of "time" now confronting us is simply part of the great eternity which He inhabits; therefore, He has already inhabited this very day. There are no surprises in it for Him. There may be for you, but there are none for Him. So, again, trust the Shepherd.

We quote here again the little chorus which we used in the beginning of this series of expositions:

My Lord knows the way through the wilderness,
    All I have to do is follow.
My Lord knows the way through the wilderness,
    All I have to do is follow.
Strength for today is mine alway
    And all I need for tomorrow.

My Lord knows the way through the wilderness,
    All I have to do is follow.

The connection between the first verse of our
psalm and the last verse is obvious. The psalm begins
and ends with the Lord. In the first verse we read,
"The LORD is my shepherd." In the last verse we
read, "I will dwell in the house of the LORD for
ever." Yes, we begin with the Lord and we are now
to dwell with Him forever. Not only does this psalm
begin and close with the Lord, but He occupies all
the space between.

Jesus Christ, our precious Shepherd, was here before there was ever human tear shed, and He will
be here when His own nail-pierced hand has wiped
the last tear from the cheek of God's blood-washed
throng.

Jesus Christ was here before ever there was a
heartache, and He'll be here when the last pang of
sorrow has moved its shadowy fingers over the
heart of one of God's anointed.

Jesus Christ was here before there was a sin, and
He will be here when the last sin and the last sinner
are locked up forever in the penitentiary of the universe, never again to escape and hurt or harm in
all of God's holy mountain.

What a glorious journey we have had in this
wonderful psalm! We began with the Shepherd. He
has taken us in every possible phase of Christian
experience, and now we are to be at home—home
with the Shepherd forever. How beautiful!

David, in another psalm, says, "This God is our
God for ever and ever: he will be our guide even

unto death" (Ps 48:14). There is a very precious truth hidden away in this verse, and it is the truth of Psalm 23. This God is our God forever! He will be our Guide until death. That is, our God is both God and Guide, but His ministry as Guide will end at the time of the pilgrim's death. He will then need no guide for he is home—safe home.

This precious truth of the relationship of the Guide to the pilgrim is brought out in stories we so often hear of guides who take individuals or parties of individuals through the Alps and other high mountain ranges. It is said that often as the guide takes his party over the treacherous mountain trail, he endears himself to his pilgrims in a very strange manner. He stops at this point and that point to call attention to some scene of magnificent beauty, and to describe it in all of its detail and significance. Then he calls the attention of his pilgrims to the fact that they are on a very dangerous stretch of road at the moment, that the path is narrow, the way is rugged, or the ravines are deep and dangerous. Another time he calls the party to a halt to point out to them how they may safely negotiate the bit of rough going ahead. Then, when it has been accomplished, a new scene of beauty bursts upon their view, and so on—up, up, up the dangerous mountainside with its changing experiences of peril, difficulty, beauty and glory until finally the journey is over and the guide has led his party safely back to the lodge below. Then comes the time for the party to pack up and say good-bye to the guide. Often these are scenes of real sadness.

How wonderful it is to know that no such experience awaits the Christian pilgrim and his wonderful Guide! Through all the days of our life our precious Shepherd has been guiding us through the wilderness, over rugged mountain passes where the going has been difficult and dark and where dangers have lurked on every hand. How sweet have been those experiences when the Shepherd has called a halt in the journey and has patiently pointed out to us how we could safely negotiate the dangerous stretch of road ahead! Then, following Him, we find ourselves suddenly through the dark shadows and into the full blaze of the sunlight of some new revelation of God's abounding grace. Then again our precious Shepherd has paused to point out the beauties and the glories of the grace of God and of His goodness to us. And so through life we have climbed the mountains, delved down into the valleys, scaled the narrow cliffs, and now comes the time when we are home, safely home. The journey is all behind us. But, unlike the experience of the mountain climber in the Alps, we do not say good-bye to our Guide, for He will be our God forever and forever!

Wonderful, blessed, sweet, eternal communion to go on and on endlessly with the one who endeared Himself to us here in these changing scenes below. Never another hill to climb. Never another dangerous mountain passage. Never another scalding, bitter tear. Never another pang of heartache and heartbreak. Never another disappointment. Gone—gone forever are these, and now, *forever, only Him.*